A Roadmap to Political Power

A Roadmap to Political Power

George Dimitroulis

Synopsis

So you want to be the next president or prime minister. What does it take to achieve this admirable goal? Well, history has repeatedly shown that successful politicians are not problem minded; they are opportunity minded. Another essential prerequisite is your ability to sell yourself. Hence, if you are an opportunist seeking to satisfy your narcissistic desires, then politics may well be your calling. All you need to know is in this book, and if you do succeed in your quest to rule the world, then make sure you mention this book, hit the like button, ring the bell, and subscribe to this channel. After all, who bothers to read books like this when it's all out there on the internet? Fortunately, for those who live in countries where internet access is tightly controlled by paranoid governments, this book is your next best thing as far as helping you climb the greasy pole to political power is concerned. So what are you waiting for? Let's get started!

Contents

PREFACE

According to Lucifer, it is better to reign in hell than to serve in heaven because the world pays attention to powerful rulers. If you want to rule – be it as president, prime minister, or even dictator – then there are a few things you must know before you reach this lofty goal. First, you need to understand the ruthless nature of politics and power because politics is a zero-sum game where there can only be one winner. Although history boasts countless examples of hedonistic power attained through force or coercion, power in modern democratic societies is largely attained by authority through persuasion, influence, and inducement. In other words, you suck up to all the people who count and kick down all those who get in your way.

Politics is about status, power, ambition, and competitiveness. In politics, power is never about doing the right thing. It is always about doing what is expedient. As U.S. president Abraham Lincoln said, 'if you want to test a man's character, give him power' as people suddenly feel entitled to treat others differently when they have power. Power simply reveals more of who they are. The ability to manipulate people's thoughts and choices is the essence of political power. To get to where you want to go isn't about brilliance but continual effort, for there is no triumph without toil. The difference you will make in the world depends a great deal on your unique talents, skills, and passions combined with opportunities. As we shall see in the pages of this book, the essential qualities required of a winning politician are as follows:

1. Mental strength
2. Determination

3. Resilience
4. A positive attitude
5. The ability to learn from failure
6. The ability to handle pressure

The way to achieve power is not to challenge the establishment but to first make a place in it amongst the powerful because you cannot change a system as an outsider. When you earn status by becoming part of the system, then you have the power to change it from within. People who seriously want to make a difference to their world recognise that politics and the power that comes with it are the only means of achieving real societal change. The other way is to demand respect through threats of violence and destruction, but this won't get you far if you end up with a cataclysmic disaster that leaves you with nothing left to rule over. Seriously though – private individuals like you and me cannot enforce law and order, build safer roads, or feed and house the destitute. It falls on responsible governments to make sure that the country is safe and prosperous and people's individual and property rights are upheld. I say 'responsible' because not all governments are the same. So unless you are fortunate enough to live in a Western-style democracy, chances are your government is unlikely to care about your individual and property rights – or anything else, for that matter. Nevertheless, political power is what makes things happen, and when it comes to making decisions, those at the top of the political pyramid wield the greatest influence. You just have to hope the guy running the show has no psychotic tendencies, and if so, pray that he takes his medication regularly. Alternatively, if you believe you have what it takes to run the biggest show in town, then the only way you can be part of the decision-making process is by climbing the greasy pole of political power. This book will tell you how.

Political power comes in many forms and is not just confined to the government. It may also be part of corporate, academic, or religious institutions where members stab one another in the back for positions of influence. While this book is largely based on the politics of sovereign nations, the principles discussed in these pages are equally applicable to political power associated with large corporations and institutions as well as professional associations and even small special interest groups.

Over many centuries, the political landscape has been cultivated by strong-willed people and random events that laid the foundations of our modern society. We will explore the various tactics used by past and present political and historical figures to achieve their goals so we get a sense of what shapes a successful ruler. Essentially, this book is about power and politics in modern society and how to achieve it in ten chapters. For those who aspire to leadership roles in the government, business, and professional associations, cancel all your appointments, find a quiet corner, and start reading. For everyone else, enjoy a light-hearted look at what makes a political leader tick.

CHAPTER 1

The How and Why of Political Power

Five hundred years ago, in a quiet farmhouse on the outskirts of Florence, a lonely, retired diplomat, Niccolò Machiavelli (1469–1527), wrote his timeless masterpiece *The Prince* in 1513, which he dedicated to Lorenzo, nephew of the reigning pope. It became a sixteenth-century classic about political power in Renaissance Italy and is still widely read by modern scholars, students, and politicians all over the world. Niccolò Machiavelli was an Italian historian who is credited as one of the main founders of modern political science. *The Prince* is a classic book about securing power by whatever means necessary. If Machiavelli lived long enough to write an updated version of his most famous book, *The Prince*, one wonders how modern history would have altered his thoughts and ideas on political power, ideas such as how a person acquires the power to rule over others, where the source of power comes from, and what abilities individuals need to acquire power, retain power, and exert power over others. To help answer these questions, we will look at the profiles of leading political figures who influenced and shaped our modern society, which provide us with a great deal of insight as to how power can be manipulated for good and evil.

There are people who moan and groan about all the injustices of the world while never getting out of their comfort zone to do something about those injustices. Gandhi said, 'Be the change you want to see in the world,' which was a rallying call to get people actively involved in changing their circumstances. Essentially, politics is the only way you can make a difference. Unfortunately, there is no job security in politics, so it takes a certain kind of person with good survival instincts to navigate the tortuous road to political power. So what does it take to be a successful politician? Many will argue that force of personality, willpower, patience, and determination are the key factors that define a good political leader. According to Descartes, those who go forward very slowly and carefully by following the right road do much better than those who are in too much haste and stray off it. Successful political leaders never seem to be in a hurry as hurrying betrays a lack of control. They always seem patient, as if they know that everything will come to them eventually. They learn to stand back when the time is not yet ripe and strike fiercely when the time is right. That is why experienced politicians accept the randomness and uncertainty of the universe and focus on things they can control. Uncertainty ensures that life will always have surprises, regardless of how carefully we plan. The more you try to be certain about something, the more insecure and uncertain you will feel. The more you embrace and accept uncertainty, the more comfortable you will feel in knowing what you don't know. Uncertainty opens your mind up to new experiences. When circumstances change, you must be able to change with them rather than slavishly sticking to your prior beliefs. Curiosity helps us to tolerate uncertainty because only the curious, who are open to learning, have a much greater chance of achieving a truly novel solution.

Political life naturally involves continual trade-offs to get what we want, and making a choice often means giving up something. For example, quality family time is often sacrificed as you move up the political ladder because there are many issues that demand a politician's attention and time. Those driven to succeed often do so at the expense of a satisfying family life. When climbing the greasy pole to power, you can improve the quality of your life by controlling your expectations. Always keep your initial expectations low and leave room to be surprised on the upside. With each experience, you take what is useful, discard the rest, and add what is uniquely your own. According to Bill Gates, success is a lousy teacher because it seduces smart people into thinking they can't lose. The only kind of success that lasts is the one that is built up slowly, and remember – all it takes is one misadventure to destroy a lifetime of success. One lovely windfall can make your day, but one nasty surprise can destroy your life. Therefore, winning is mostly about not losing.

Many years ago, Desiderius Erasmus said that 'in the land of the blind, the one-eyed man is king'. What he meant was that those with a natural advantage command the most influence. It makes you wonder how a blind community would trust the guy with the one working eye, but I suppose they have no choice but to follow the one who is blessed with the vision. If you are the guy with the one eye, then you already have a natural advantage that you need to exploit. Few of us ever become truly exceptional at more than one thing – if anything at all. So you need to find what you are good at and where your natural talent lies and work from there. Whatever it is you are passionate about is probably the same thing that you'll be really good at. The factors that make you successful are your talent and your drive. Success comes to those who can appreciate their unique qualities and select vocations in the areas they are best at. Follow your passions and natural strengths, which will guide you to your most fulfilling career. If you are blessed with good social skills, then politics may well be your calling. The big choices we make in life are practically random; however, it is the small choices that tell us more about who we are. The fact that you are a politician, for example, is not very revealing, but what kind of politician you become may reflect deep traits. There are plenty of politicians but very few who make it to the pinnacle of power, so winning elections does not guarantee that you will ever reach the top. To survive long term, it is better to see politics as something you do rather than who you are. People who look for purpose in their work are more successful in pursuing their passions and less likely to quit their jobs than those who look for glory.

Your first step on the road to political power requires an understanding of what politics is all about and how political power works. As previously mentioned, to attain political power, you need to appreciate that the real world is unpredictable and full of surprises. Achieving excellence in school often requires mastering old ways of thinking, but building an influential career in politics demands new ways of thinking. To succeed, you must be willing to learn and adjust as you go and even to abandon a previous goal and change directions entirely should the need arise. It is far more helpful to assume that you're ignorant and don't know a whole lot as it promotes a constant state of learning and growth. There is no master key that will unlock all doors. The knowledge we obtain through real-life experience is vastly superior to the knowledge obtained through reasoning. If you have the passion and energy, you need focus and direction to succeed. You need real-world experience because for every leader who has succeeded in rising to the pinnacle of power, there are dozens of equally hard-working, competent individuals who have tried and failed and fallen by the wayside. So how do the few succeed where many others have failed? Read on.

Power belongs to a cohesive group who empower individuals to act in their name. While the group shape preferences and set the agenda, the decision making is the prerogative of those at the apex of the pyramid of political power. Power is concentrated in just a few hands, and your goal is to make sure one of those hands is yours because what you want is the power to shape and drive the international, national, corporate, or even group agenda, depending on where you end up. Doors may open in ways unforeseen for your unique contribution to be expressed. Fate may throw us many obstacles and opportunities during our lifetimes. The trick is how we react to them. For the lucky ones blessed with resilience and fortitude, opportunities favour the prepared, and obstacles merely create challenges for those determined to get ahead in life regardless of their background. For the weak and vulnerable, opportunities remain invisible, and obstacles become insurmountable barriers that reinforce their debility. The difference between success and failure is that bad luck is always the excuse used by those who have failed in life. Timing and luck make the greatest difference between obscurity and success – Napoleon's rise to power was made possible by the French Revolution. If Hitler lived in a different era, would he have achieved the same destructive power? World War II gave Churchill the break he needed to cement his place in history. In short, the course of history gave them their opportunity, and they took it. They all had the great good fortune to be born at a time and in circumstances when they could make use of their unique talents.

In any society, influence means power, and politics is essentially the expression of power and influence in a society. While legitimate political power is held by heads of sovereign nations, it is not always transparent and propitious. It can be used for good and evil. Dysfunctional societies arise when interactions are exploitative, so that trust is destroyed. You cannot transplant a political culture of democracy and freedom to a place where there is no topsoil of trust. Where there is no trust, people will end up cooperating under a repressive system of formal rules and regulations which are enforced by coercive means. People who want to change the society in which they live have three main choices. One is to terrorise their neighbours and hold their fellow human beings to ransom, like al-Qaeda or the Irish Republican Army (IRA). Another way is to pay off all the important individuals and groups to do their dirty work, just like the

Italian Mafia do when they pay magistrates and the police to turn a blind eye to their illegal activities. Essentially, insurgencies, terrorist groups, and multinational corporations can also wield significant influence on societies, effectively giving them the power to dictate their own terms and conditions.

You may have guessed that terror and corruption are like a cancer on society. They destroy the very fabric of community life and tear apart social order and justice, which simply means your power is like a terminal disease that eventually kills you. For those sensible enough to shun the temptation of malevolence, the only legitimate way to power is to run for political office on a platform of policies that will benefit your fellow man. Legitimate power is supported by fair and free elections run by the people for the benefit of the people. Otherwise, as an illegitimate ruler, you run the real risk of incarceration or cold-blooded execution, and so you have little choice but to rule for life and constantly watch your back just to stay alive. Therefore, it is wise and much safer to be a legitimate ruler so that you can confidently step down from high office with a lifetime pension rather than lifetime imprisonment or death.

Forging lasting relationships, even with difficult people, is a key advantage of political aspirants who want to get ahead in their pursuit of political power. People marry for the same reasons countries trade – comparative advantage – because each partner has something the other wants, so there is a 'win-win' outcome for both parties. In other words, you have no chance of ever achieving power if you don't willingly make concessions and do not follow the 'win-win' principle. Besides being an easy-going and agreeable person, you need to be out there 'spruiking' your talents and reminding people what a great guy you are no matter how many speeding fines, sexual assault charges, and bankruptcies you have accumulated in your life. In fact, a chequered past does not necessarily disqualify you from high office if you can gather enough sympathy from your sob story about turning your life around. After all, U.S. president Bill Clinton's voracious sexual appetite did little to hurt his public approval ratings. Powerbrokers sometimes see the value in singling out colourful characters for the top prize because the public are more likely to remember candidates with an interesting past than squeaky-clean candidates who have no life experiences to bring to the post of a potential leader. If you haven't failed at anything, it means that you haven't stepped out of your comfort zone, and you are unlikely to ever reach your full potential.

———

The struggle for political power is a game of brinkmanship where people select candidates who best satisfy their own selfish needs. Selfish people ask, 'What's in it for me?' In a leadership battle, the victors are those who can most effectively lie and manipulate incentives (i.e. beliefs, costs, and outcomes) so that people are swayed to choose leaders who appear to best fulfil their desires for a better life. It doesn't matter if the promises cannot be delivered if it caters to what people want to hear, such as prosperity without enormous personal cost. We all know the cost of prosperity is indeed very high because free universal education and healthcare, for example, come at a cost of punishingly high taxes. Hopeful politicians wanting to gain power through election know that empty promises are simply a means to an end, and shrewd politicians know how to cleverly exploit them as tricks of the trade, which we will see later.

In an election, never underestimate your opponents and always hold on to the fear of defeat because those who stand to lose will fight harder than those who stand to gain. Winning an election is always a team effort because losing is when a team play like individuals. While unity in your party is key to winning elections, you are unlikely to win anything simply by following the formula of another winner. If you do the same as them, they win because they've been doing it for longer. Matching what your opponent has to offer distracts your resources away from what you're best at and what you are best known for. You need to stay ahead of the game by doing something unique rather than reacting to what they have already done. If your policy decisions are purely reactive, you will be playing your opponent's game. Successful politicians thrive on change, on improvement, on updating and upgrading their ability to survive a changing environment. A political party that can never be changed has within its DNA the seeds of its own extinction.

Political power also depends on the individual and the circumstances surrounding their ascent to power. Circumstances like revolution, war, famine, or economic crises can have a tremendous bearing on an anxious population desperate for a way out of their predicament. A nation's history is shaped by their leaders, whose power can embolden them to make decisions that benefit their subjects or corrupt those who use it to bolster their own interests. Everyone has an incomplete view of the world, and the way to make sense of it is that they try and fill it with their own narratives. The hardest thing to accept is how much of what happens in the world is out of our control. So we turn to authoritative-sounding people who fulfil our need to believe that we live in a predictable and controllable world.

That is where dysfunctional political leaders step in because they understand that the illusion of control is more persuasive than the reality of uncertainty. The moment a ruler tries to achieve the perfection of 'one view' of how things should be is when things start to go bad. It all depends on the narrative dished out by the leadership, which often portrays an external threat as the perpetrator of the nation's woes, and the heroes battling these threats are the valiant leaders of their own nation. No one ever cares to mention the possibility that perhaps a country's problems may well be emblematic of the nation's own political system. Crucially, the finger pointing is often directed at other entities, groups, or even foreign powers who are to blame for everything, from poor water quality to a fractured health system that is struggling to provide even the basic healthcare needs of the population. Shifting the blame is a clever decoy used by adroit politicians who manage to survive from one crisis to the next.

If countries want long-term stability and prosperity, they need to get their political system in order first. For a political system to function, it requires trust and faith in those who are being governed. In Western nations, the reason you go into politics is to make a better society. In poverty-stricken nations, you go into politics to get rich. To appreciate the merits of Western democracy, we need to take a detailed look at failed states that are ruled by despotic dictators. States which attempt to exploit or deny their populations rights are vulnerable to uprising. When large numbers of people withdraw their cooperation from an oppressive system, the odds are in their favour for change. Failed political institutions and endemic corruption are what all developing countries have in common. The disintegration of weak states in Africa and the Middle East is creating large emerging zones of disorder and chaos, which threatens the stability of world order. Violent insurgencies depend on young violence-prone unemployed and disenfranchised males who are prone to ongoing conflict and corruption. Sadly, many developing nations today are still ruled by despotic and sordid dictators whose power is based on the threat of violence and supported by brutality and corruption. Power through force and coercion is precarious at best for leaders who presume they can subdue their people forever.

The 2011 uprising in the Middle East that swept through Egypt,

Libya, Tunisia, Yemen, and Syria is testament to the determination of its people to rid their respective nations of autocratic rulers who selfishly plundered their country's riches for their own benefit. Alas, power gained and maintained by violence often ends in violence, as proved by the ignominious demise of Libya's brutal dictator, Colonel Gaddafi, after four decades of repressive rule. Removing tyrants from power sometimes leads to freedom but occasionally may result in a new form of tyranny if the population remains disorganised. Nothing can be achieved without proper organisation. Good organisation is the fundamental key to power because most revolutions simply substitute one ruling class for another since it is often the army and not the people that instigates the toppling of a dictator, whom they often replace with another dictator. The army simply stands back and encourages the people to overthrow the government and then steps back into the fray to install a new leader.

Corruption is the tool of power and the bedrock of absolute dictatorship. Corruption declines as a country moves from dictatorship to democracy as leaders become more accountable to more people and politics becomes a competition for good ideas, not bribes and corruption. Dictators impose harsh taxes on their unproductive population as they need to keep their treasury topped up and do not rely on their citizens for power. Democracies, on the other hand, have very productive populations, and so taxes are lower, and the wages are higher as their power relies on the people, who must be kept happy. Democracy works best in an educated population who can distinguish between right and wrong, where the voters know how the world works, so they can make intelligent policy choices and are less likely to fall prey to misleading demagogues, ideological zealots, or conspiracy buffs. Unfortunately, history has demonstrated all too often that elected leaders can take advantage of their poorly educated population to wrest control of the democratic process and turn elections into a farcical exercise in self-promotion. Robert Mugabe's Zimbabwe is a perfect case in point.

As a leader of the liberation movement against white-minority rule, Robert Gabriel Mugabe (1924–2019) was elected into power in 1980 and served as prime minister (PM) from 1980 to 1987 and then president from 1987 to 2017. His successful re-elections conveniently followed the dictator's rulebook of widespread intimidation, election fraud, and vote rigging. During his thirty-seven-year rule, Zimbabwe went from the breadbasket of the African continent to a basket case of African nations as his poor judgement and erratic behaviour resulted in hyperinflation and total economic collapse. Mugabe's appalling brutal repression, economic mismanagement, and blatant corruption made him a poster boy for African dictators ostracised by many of the world's leaders as a pariah. His abuse of human rights and abject disregard for the democratic process in Zimbabwe resulted in economic sanctions as well as travel bans by many Western nations for all Zimbabwean ministers, including Mugabe himself. His wife, Grace, was subject to fierce criticism for her lavish European shopping sprees in the face of catastrophic poverty blighting the people of Zimbabwe. You can't blame her for spending the Zimbabwean treasury funds overseas as her husband left her with no shops back home. Sadly, it is the first world banking system that supports and permits the siphoning of illegal funds by corrupt African leaders from their people into personal Swiss bank accounts.

Dictators don't just want to change the world; they want to totally transform it through censorship, repression, and violence. Successful dictators surround themselves with trusted friends, clans, and family. To keep a strong hold on power, a dictator must occasionally purge his key supporters to keep them to a minimum, making them easier to control. After all, too many key supporters are harder to control as the rewards are spread too thinly and there is a greater chance of being toppled by a revolution. For dictators, it is the key supporters they need to keep happy and not the mass population, who, as far as they are concerned, can go hungry. For a power-hungry leader in a dysfunctional political system, it is always better for him to determine who eats than it is to have a larger pie from which people can feed themselves. In a dictatorship, you pay your key supporters just enough to keep them loyal and remove those who are ambitious enough to threaten your leadership. Hence, the three golden rules of absolute power are as follows:

1. No man rules alone. They must rely on key supporters to help keep them in power.
2. To maintain the loyalty of the few key supporters, you must reward them well.
3. To be able to pay for the loyalty, you must have full control of your treasury.

To survive in power, dictators must keep their population hungry, poorly educated, and ignorant and their treasury full to pay off all those who keep them in power, like the army and police. Poorly educated, hungry, and ignorant peasants do not have the energy and know-how to revolt against their oppressive government, especially a government that is threatening and coercive. Occasionally, a natural disaster will be an opportunity for dysfunctional rulers to fill their treasury coffers. Governments of poor countries may deliberately obstruct the flow of immediate overseas aid following a natural disaster so that the body count can rise sufficiently for dictators to attract much more aid than if aid agencies were given immediate access that could have prevented further deaths. Once the body count is high enough following earthquakes and floods, the dictators eventually throw open their disaster-stricken countries to overseas aid agencies by slapping tariffs on the aid itself to help fill their treasury coffers. I'm not kidding!

Long-term power results in growing arrogance and a sense of entitlement, with reason and compassion as the major casualties. History is replete with examples of how absolute power can warp people's minds and be used for evil purposes. In early human history, there were some seriously scary dudes whose power was often exercised through coercion or the threat of force. Ivan the Terrible (1530–1584), the sixteenth-century tsar of Russia, ruled his kingdom with an iron fist, and his power became synonymous with cruelty and terror. While the early part of his rule was largely successful and prosperous for his people, he increasingly became mentally unstable in his later years, which, incidentally, is not uncommon in leaders who appoint themselves rulers for life. As a measure of his cruelty, in 1581, he struck his pregnant daughter-in-law and killed her husband, who came to her aid, who, by the way, was also named Ivan, his son and heir. This would have obviously made a big impact in his succession planning, but luckily, he had other less defensive offspring to choose from.

When he was crowned the first tsar of Russia in 1547 at the age of just 16 years old, Ivan became the absolute ruler. He became the 'divine' leader appointed to enact God's will, which is another way of saying that 'you don't f**k with him'. Ivan's legacy was to convert an absolutist political arrangement into a repressive dictatorship. Ivan successfully centralised the government in Russia through autocratic rule and, in the process, also established a centralised system of political control in the shape of his own guard. Thus, the entire course of Russian history has been dominated by the political guard that has become another dreadful legacy of Ivan the

Terrible. The idea of a guard as a means of political control became so entrenched in Russian history that centuries later, Joseph Stalin had no reservations in placing the guard or political police force between himself and the party.

The remorseless and brutal Soviet leader Joseph Stalin is an extraordinary example of how absolute power corrupts absolutely. Joseph Vissarionovich Stalin (1878–1953) was the first general secretary of the Communist Party of the Soviet Union from 1922 and premier from 6 May 1941 until his death on 5 March 1953. He was amongst the Bolshevik revolutionaries who brought about the October Revolution in 1917, and after Vladimir Lenin's death in 1924, Stalin brutally put down all opposition groups and managed to consolidate more and more power in his hands. Under Stalin's direction, a period of rapid economic and social changes took place where millions of people, including many political convicts, were deported and exiled to penal labour camps in remote areas of the Soviet Union. In his efforts to change the Soviet Union from an agrarian to an industrial power, the initial upheaval in the changing agricultural sector disrupted food production in the early 1930s, contributing to the catastrophic Soviet famine of 1932–1933, where countless millions died. Stalin, as head of the politburo, consolidated near-absolute power in the 1930s with a 'Great Purge' of the party, justified as an attempt to expel 'counter-revolutionary infiltrators'.

The Great Purge of 1937–1938 ushered in a brutal campaign against alleged enemies of the regime, such as former members of the communist opposition and potential rivals in the party, in which hundreds of thousands of people were executed, including Red Army leaders convicted of treason. Those targeted by the purge were expelled from the party, banished to the Gulag labour camps, or executed after sham trials. The repression of so many formerly high-ranking revolutionaries and party members was testament to Stalin's intense suspicion and paranoia, which gave him a tight grip on power at all costs, power that he would only relinquish upon his death. From 1929 to 1953, it is estimated that more than fourteen million people passed through the Gulag, with a further eight million people deported and exiled to remote areas of the Soviet Union (including entire nationalities), which profoundly affected the ethnic map of the Soviet Union. Official records obtained from the Soviet archives retrieved after the 1991 dissolution of the Soviet Union contained evidence of the execution of approximately 800,000 prisoners under Stalin for either political or criminal offenses, some 390,000 deaths during kulak forced resettlement, and around 1.7 million deaths in the Gulags. In all, historians have estimated twenty million deaths attributable to Stalin, which included famine victims.

Stalin was a truly evil man who knew his purpose, extending and consolidating his ruthless power by exterminating those with leadership ambitions who would threaten his tight-fisted grip on power. He was a tough negotiator and a man of few words, not because he was dyslexic but more because his evil crimes said it all. Uncle Joe discovered that plying his closest political advisers with lots of alcohol loosened their tongues so that he could extract information that would feed his paranoia. He trusted no one, and no one trusted him, so his ignominious end was no surprise as lots of people closest to him wanted him dead before they themselves were exterminated by the whims of this crazed psychopath. It is little wonder that Stalin's successor, Nikita Khrushchev, denounced his legacy, but modern views of Stalin in the Russian Federation remain mixed, with some viewing him as the architect of Soviet supremacy following World War II. There is little doubt that Joseph Stalin will go down in history as one of mankind's ugliest examples of misuse of power that was exploited for immoral purposes.

A nation's prosperity is vital to its political stability. In desperate times, however, nations look to leaders who promise everything, regardless of whether they can deliver. It is often not surprising to see, in a country of high unemployment and poverty – given the choice between a prudent leader imploring his people to make short-term sacrifices for the long-term good and a reckless leader who promises jobs and riches now – how impoverished people will vote. In desperate situations, we abandon our deeply held beliefs and moral values in our desire to belong to a group with a different set of values and beliefs who promise a way out of our own misery. If we pander to bad people who promise falsehoods, we willingly become their victims, and the world will be run by them. This perhaps may explain the rise of Nazi Germany, where the whole population abandoned its morals and scruples to blindly follow a deluded leader hellbent on war and world domination as his aim. Voltaire presciently wrote that 'those who can make you believe absurdities can make you commit atrocities'. A reliable way to make people believe in falsehoods is frequent repetitions because familiarity is not easily distinguished from truth. People are more likely to be influenced by persuasive messages when they are tired or depleted. This scenario, unfortunately, is repeated all over the world, where desperate populations seek miraculous saviours and almost always end up with brutal dictators who deliver more pain and hardships.

The rise of Adolf Hitler (1889–1945) was boosted by the misery of vulnerable German people who were looking for a saviour from their crushing debt levels, high unemployment, and hyperinflation that had gripped their country following its defeat in World War I. Scholars often regard the period of the Great Depression in the early 1930s as the seed that brought Hitler to power. Even though Hitler lost the elections of 1932, he exploited the population's discontent and managed to curtail Hindenburg's power and have himself installed as chancellor in January 1933. By March, Hitler succeeded in transforming his new government into a de facto dictatorship. When President Hindenburg died in August 1934, Hitler quickly moved to combine the presidency with the chancellorship, effectively making him the absolute ruler of Germany. He achieved this by flouting the constitution to remove all institutional checks and balances on his power, which effectively removed the last legal avenue by which Hitler could be dismissed. In the pre-war years, Hitler oversaw one of the largest infrastructure improvement campaigns in German history. Unemployment fell dramatically as people were put to work constructing dams, highways (autobahns), railroads, and other civil works. The main driver of increased economic activity, however, was the expansion of the military, mostly through arms production.

It seemed the Nazi Party had fulfilled its promise to improve the lives of the German people through work and industrial prosperity. This placed Hitler in a strong position to command admiration and total discipline from his people, who faithfully and blindly adhered to his warped ideology. By early 1938, Hitler had asserted his control of the military-foreign policy apparatus and assumed the role and title of the supreme commander of the armed forces. From that moment onward, Hitler pursued a foreign policy that had war as its aim. From the invasion of Poland in September 1939 to his suicide on 30 April 1945, Hitler's orders resulted in the deaths of approximately forty million people in calamitous events that embroiled the world in the Second World War. Sadly, the world will never be free of tyrants and brutal dictators as long as there are economic hardships and poorly organised masses who succumb to the false ideology of malevolent leaders.

While this book is intended for those seeking power by legitimate means, it is important to consider the above examples of how absolute power can be corrupting to those who wield it and destructive to the population that suffers the appalling repercussions of absolute rule. In this chapter, we looked at examples of notorious political leaders who epitomised how power can be abused for evil purposes, resulting in hardships and sorrow for the people subjected to their rule. It seems that the rule of law meant nothing to these tyrants, and each was able to manipulate the nation's constitution to consolidate absolute power in their favour. The confounding concern with malevolent leadership is how such deranged figures managed to attain absolute power in the first place. Surely, the population could see beyond the facade of strong leadership and recognise the malicious character by the immoral actions perpetrated upon them. Alas, the sad truth is that many people do indeed see the immorality of criminal political leaders, but those brave enough to speak out are swiftly silenced by detention or death. Rather than being lionised as heroes, they are branded as traitors, and their terrible fate is made an example of what may happen if others speak out against the 'state or its leader'.

Fortunately, autocratic rule is rarely tolerated in a modern democracy because those leaders who constantly ignore the opinion and advice of others become increasingly isolated. History has shown that absolute rulers lose their sense of reality and invariably follow a destructive path that has negative repercussions for their nation. Tragically, opposition dissent, freedom of the press, and individual liberties are all casualties of absolute rule. For instance, when journalists are free to write about the hardships of the poor, the government has an incentive to do something about it. Without press freedom, totalitarian regimes can commit whatever atrocities serve their agenda. The checks and balances that frame the constitutions of prosperous nations ensure that these nations are spared from the tyrannies of absolute power in the hands of a few individuals. In Machiavelli's time, political power was often achieved through violence and corruption, which is in stark contrast to the idiosyncrasies of democracy in the modern state, where political leaders must negotiate their power to rule.

***

One of the major pitfalls of political leadership is that the president or PM not only takes all the credit but also cops the blame for policies and legislation that is effectively not their own but someone else's idea.

Leaders rely heavily on their inner circle of deputies for ideas and advice because their heavy work commitments give them precious little time to think for themselves. There are too many distractions for leaders to come up with original ideas of their own, so they spend their leadership years seeking advice and making decisions based on the advice they receive. If the advice is bad, the leadership will suffer. The caucus and the president's team, therefore, have an important obligation to ensure that leaders get the right advice.

While leadership is the ultimate power, you can still wield plenty of power as a high-ranking official. If you want to make a real impact in the world of politics, you need a high-ranking position in a mainstream political party, which does not necessarily involve leadership of the party. It may be a deputy or party whip, house speaker or senate majority leader, secretary of state, or even foreign minister. As long as you are within the inner circle of the president or PM, your power and influence are considerably strong. Having the ear of the president is safer than being the president as your power is hidden behind the facade of your leader. That way, while you may not be bathed in the spotlight of glory when things are going well, you will at least avoid the onslaught of malicious attacks and arrows of criticism when things are not doing so well. Minor parties and independents are simply fringe dwellers who occasionally hold the balance of power in a hung parliament. The Labour front bench minister, Peter Garrett, obviously recognised this when he entered the political arena as a Labour Party member, even though his natural allegiance lay with the Greens. He rightly figured that if he was to make a difference in the world of politics, he would need to align himself with one of the major parties. His aim was not to be leader but to be as close as possible to the leader. He clearly recognised that the closer you are to the leader, the louder your voice becomes.

Incredible as it may seem, senior ministers and congressmen can wield immense power through their influence and persuasiveness. There are many politicians who command enormous power but are more comfortable out of the limelight. Factional heavyweights who work behind the scenes can easily engineer the rise and fall of political leaders. Ministers have the advantage of not being encumbered by the burdens of high office and have more time to think about policies and government affairs. While leaders are hosting or attending various events that leaders are obliged to do for the sake of keeping up appearances, senior party officials and ministers can get on with the business of power and running the government.

So if you want to make a difference in politics without being in the spotlight, perhaps it may be better to leave the top job to narcissists and concentrate on the real job of running government as a cabinet minister or congressman. As the long-time faithful deputy of the British PM Winston Churchill, Anthony Eden made a lasting contribution to the war effort, even though his critical role was completely overshadowed by his world-famous boss. Robert Anthony Eden, First Earl of Avon (1897–1977), was Britain's Conservative PM from 1955 to 1957. His greatest political achievements were three stints as foreign secretary, between 1935 and 1955, especially during the Second World War, under Winston Churchill's leadership.

Before he became PM, Eden had a worldwide reputation as an opponent of appeasement, a 'man of peace', and a skilled diplomat. His experiences of having served in the First World War made Eden strongly anti-war and an ardent supporter of peace in Europe. However, he recognised that peace could not be maintained by appeasement of the Axis powers, Nazi Germany and fascist Italy, who were spoiling for a fight. On the outbreak of war in September 1939, Eden became secretary of state for dominion affairs in Neville Chamberlain's government. However, because he was not in the war cabinet, Eden missed his first real opportunity for the premiership when Chamberlain resigned after Germany invaded France in May 1940 and Churchill became PM. Eden was one of Churchill's closest confidants and served loyally as Churchill's lieutenant in his plumb position of secretary of state for war, where he played a critical supporting role during World War II. In 1945, Eden went into opposition as deputy leader of the Conservative Party after the shock defeat of Churchill's caretaker Conservative government by the Labour Party of Clement Attlee, who broke off the wartime coalition government at the end of the European war in May 1945.

It was at this time that many felt that Churchill should have retired and allowed Eden to become party leader. However, Churchill refused to consider stepping down, and Eden's loyalty fuelled Churchill's determination to hold on as leader. In any case, 1945 was a tragic time for Eden, who endured the personal loss of his son and breakup of his first marriage and was in no mood to contest a leadership challenge. In opposition, Churchill was only a part-time leader given his many journeys abroad and pursuit of other interests and left the day-to-day work of government largely to Eden. Eden took this opportunity to acquaint himself with domestic affairs and establish a handle of what the common man on the street desired when he came up with the idea of the 'property-owning democracy' that Margaret Thatcher adopted many decades later.

When the Conservatives returned to office in 1951 and Churchill became PM once again, Eden became foreign secretary for the third time. As in opposition, Eden continued his de facto leadership duties as deputy PM while the ailing Churchill relished his return to power, albeit as a figurehead in his government. This time, Eden had effective control of British foreign policy for the first time as he oversaw the decline of the British Empire and escalation of the Cold War. Although Britain was no longer the world power it had been before the war, Eden achieved a great deal by successfully dealing with various international crises in his third term in the foreign office. After intense pressure from his own cabinet, Churchill finally retired in April 1955, and Eden finally succeeded him as PM.

As soon as he became PM, Eden called a general election, which gave him and his Conservative government a substantially increased majority from seventeen to sixty seats. As PM, Eden shunned domestic matters and focused on the foreign office. His poor experience in economic matters and tight control of the foreign office drew widespread criticism, and he was ultimately forced to stand down less than two years as leader, citing health reasons. What finally precipitated his downfall was the Suez Crisis in 1956, where Britain secretly colluded with France and Israel to wrest back control of the Suez Canal, which was nationalised by Nasser and brought under Egyptian control. Fearing a Soviet backlash, the U.S. ambassador Henry Cabot Lodge Jr. pressed for an immediate withdrawal at the United Nations (UN), thereby rendering the operation a complete failure. Eden's reputation as a revered statesman was ruined by the Suez fiasco, which signalled the end of British dominance in the Middle East, and he tendered his resignation as PM on 9 January 1957.

Although he is generally ranked amongst the least successful British PMs of the twentieth century, Eden retained much of his personal popularity in Britain and was created Earl of Avon in 1961. Despite his poor leadership skills, Eden's achievements during his long tenure as deputy made him a very popular political figure even in retirement. His limited success as leader would have no doubt been compounded by his shyness and lack of self-confidence, which was evident in his poor performance as a public speaker and chairing cabinet meetings, something his old boss Winston Churchill was supremely adept at. Sadly, history will always remember Anthony Eden as the most ineffectual British PM of the twentieth century, and yet if he had remained a loyal deputy without ever having become leader, history would have looked back on his accomplishments in a more positive light, albeit as a footnote to great leaders such as Winston Churchill.

On occasions, power resides in the deputy, and leaders are simply the public face of the party, as was plainly the case when Dmitry Medvedev took over the Russian presidency while Vladimir Putin stepped aside, for constitutional reasons, to take on the PM's role in 2008. It was clear to the Americans after 2008 that Putin was still in charge when it came to nuclear arms negotiations, even though Medvedev was president and head of state. After a single brief tense meeting with Putin in 2009, U.S. president Obama steered clear of the Russian PM and only conversed with President Medvedev, a more amiable person who understood and respected other viewpoints. Putin is a tough negotiator, and his steely reserve made him a difficult man to do business with. So it is no surprise that even as PM, Putin still ran the country from behind the scenes until he regained the presidency once again in 2012 and is now president for life.

Today's Queen of England, while head of state, is only a figurehead with vastly diminished powers which have devolved over the centuries from the hereditary monarchy to the elected parliament for very good reasons. Hereditary power does not ensure competence. History is replete with examples of ineffectual rulers who ascended to the seat of power through birth right. Their rule was effectively the product of close advisors and royal ministers who wielded the power behind the monarch. These were the faceless men and women who had the ear of the ruling monarch and cleverly used their privileged positions to influence decisions made by the ruling king or queen. Power resided in the royal court and was commensurate with the competence of the ruling monarch. The weaker the king, the stronger the power that lay in the hands of his ministers and advisors. No one remembers the deputy, but this may not be a bad thing because when things go bad, the ruler gets the blame, while the deputy may escape unnoticed. However, this wasn't always the case, as we shall see with the life and times of the most famous of English monarchs, King Henry VIII.

King Henry VIII (1491–1547) was King of England from 1509 until his death in 1547. Henry was the second monarch of the House of Tudor, succeeding his father, King Henry VII, whose eldest son died before he could accede to the throne. In his youth, Henry was a handsome and charismatic figure, well educated, and an accomplished author and composer. During the course of his life, he became harsh, egotistical, and lustful as his public image suffered from his insecurities, morbid obesity, and declining health. While Henry VIII is best remembered for his six wives, his struggles with Rome led to the separation of the Church of England from papal authority, and he established himself as the head of the Church of England. The English Reformation made England a largely Protestant nation under Henry's rule. When Henry first ascended the throne, he relied heavily on advisors until his confidence matured, and he eventually ruled with absolute power.

The Catholic cardinal Thomas Wolsey (1473–1530) served the young king from 1514 to 1529 as the lord chancellor and controlled both domestic and foreign policy. It was Wolsey who forged alliances with France and the Holy Roman Empire and forced loans from the rich to pay for foreign wars. Wolsey also centralised the national government. Unfortunately for Wolsey, he not only angered the rich with his ostentatious lifestyle when the treasury was empty but also upset the king when he failed to secure a quick divorce from Queen Catherine. After sixteen years as the king's faithful deputy, he was stripped of his powers in 1529, was arrested on false charges of treason, and died in custody a year later. His ignominious end was a terse reminder that while deputies can wield immense power and influence, unhappy rulers can just as easily suspend that power on a whim.

While Henry took full control of his government and ruled with absolute power, scholars argue that he was distracted by his own domestic affairs (i.e. six wives) and obsession to produce a male heir to take direct control of the nation's affairs for any extended period. The king was intelligent and shrewd, but most importantly, he relied on others for most of his ideas and to do most of the work. It seems that much of the positive outcomes that emerged during the reign of King Henry VIII can be credited as the work of Thomas Cromwell (1485–1540). Amongst other things, Cromwell conceived the commonwealth of England that included popular participation through parliament and parliamentary consent, which gradually eroded the monarch's power – but not while Henry VIII remained on the throne. Sadly, Cromwell also succumbed to the fury of his king and was executed in 1540 after he engineered a disastrous marital union between Henry and a very unattractive German princess, Anne of Cleves. Unfortunately, being a very competent and capable minister and advisor counted for little in King Henry's court when one upsets His Royal Highness.

So being a faithful and very capable deputy can sometimes have its drawbacks, especially when serving under absolute rulers with short memories and highly volatile temperaments. Joseph Stalin, our leading contender for the cruellest ruler ever, made sure that none of his deputies came too close to his power base and eliminated anyone who appeared vaguely threatening to his grip on power. Stalin's insecurities demonstrated how powerful good deputies can be and how much of a threat they can pose when weak leaders assume the reins of power. Often senior political figures wield considerable power and influence behind the scenes and can easily make or break leadership aspirations. So political power is not simply about leadership. Therefore, if your aim is for political power without the glory, the position of party whip, senior minister, senator, or congressman may just be the job for you. That way, your power and influence come without the baggage and burdens of leadership.

Now that you understand what political power is all about, let's explore what it takes to successfully navigate the long and tortuous roadmap to political power and how to hold on to power once you get to the top. The road to political power is long and hard, but to hold on to power, as we shall see, is even harder.

Chapter 2

Appearance and the Media

In 1960, there was a now famous televised debate between U.S. presidential hopefuls John Kennedy and Richard Nixon. Apart from being the first ever televised debate in U.S. history, it demonstrated something completely unexpected. The debate clearly showed the importance of appearance when post-debate polling showed that while Nixon won the debate for radio listeners, television viewers thought otherwise and placed Kennedy as the winner. Political analysts suggested that Kennedy's good looks swayed TV viewers, which helped amplified his message and attract positive responses from audiences who saw the debate as opposed to those who only listened to it on radio. Nixon had the advantage of having been vice president to Eisenhower in the eight years prior to the debate, so he had a much stronger position and was better known to the public than Kennedy. A successfully established politician like Nixon is more likely to win an election than an unknown candidate like Kennedy, even though Kennedy subsequently won the presidential race by the narrowest of margins, thanks largely to his father's deep pockets and some questionable deals done behind the scenes. Perhaps his good looks also helped. Hence, in an election, a sitting member trying to retain his seat will have the advantage over his rivals in terms of political experience and public recognition, which makes it very difficult for newcomers to enter the political arena. That's why your first step on the road to power is to be noticed.

Everything at first glance is judged by its appearance because what is unseen counts for nothing. Attractive people manage to climb higher in their chosen professions than their less attractive peers. It is well known that attractive and well-groomed people are also more likely to secure a job offer, all else being equal. Well-groomed individuals have a big advantage over their unsightly compatriots and can find themselves in enviable positions very early in their political careers. People with poor grooming habits must work harder to gain a foothold in the world of politics. In a world where voters have plenty of choices, aspiring politicians need to compete for attention. In a crowded political arena, you rarely get a second chance to make a first impression, so physical appearance plays a large part in the evaluation of candidates. What first sets people apart is their appearance, and looks can go a long way to securing friendships and favours. Attention is what you need to rise above the crowd, and there is no better way to be spotted than when you look your best – and looking your best doesn't mean looking different from everyone else. Politics is a conservative arena that does not reward outrageous individuality like you would see on the red carpet of the entertainment world. The 'Kardashian' road show is all about trying to be different to influence styles and fashions amongst a well-defined demographic cohort. Politics, on the other hand, needs to appeal to a very broad cross-section of society, so your individual style and appearance must fall well within the boundaries of boring but elegant and tasteful. Politics is one of the few areas where old age is a clear advantage, so a prospective politician with a baby face and youthful appearance has little hope of gaining traction as the voting public equates age to experience. Experience is what everyone looks for in a leader, although U.S. voters may have taken this a little to the extreme with U.S. president Joe Biden, who was inaugurated at the ripe old age of 79 years old.

While good grooming habits give you a head start, they cannot be relied on for political survival if beauty is only skin deep and folly is in your blood. Take the example of U.S. president Warren G. Harding (1865–1923), whose rule was cut short when he died in office of a heart attack in 1923 while only having served a little over two years as president. As a young man, he was spotted and courted by Washington powerbrokers who commented that he would make a very handsome president indeed, and indeed, he did, thanks largely to his backers. Unfortunately, Harding's good looks did not translate to good deeds, and his presidency was tainted by scandals, so much so that Harding has gone down in the record books as one of the worst U.S. presidents in modern times.

In the modern world, where the media paints the political landscape, it pays to concentrate on your physical appearance as often the voting public are more likely to pay attention to what a handsome movie star has to say about poverty in Africa (a.k.a. George Clooney) than what a bald reserve bank governor has to say about the state of the U.S. economy. Why is it that television news readers are invariably attractive? Television executives obviously believe that people are more likely to tune in to an attractive newsreader at the helm. On the international stage, the pride and dignity of a country are represented in every leader's appearance, and public relations people ensure that their sartorially pleasing leader stands out in a positive light when lined up with other leaders for the obligatory photoshoot on the world stage.

Sir Les Paterson – the alter ego of Australia's most famous expatriate entertainer, Barry Humphries – nicely encapsulates the importance of appearance. Sir Les, while only a fictional character, underscores the value of good grooming habits in public figures by highlighting how repulsive individuals can be if the state of their physical appearance is totally neglected. While his general appearance is repugnant, the effect is accentuated by the vile appearance of his foul teeth. One should never underestimate the value of an attractive smile in all political leaders who are in the media spotlight. For those not privileged with perfect white teeth, there is a whole dental industry devoted to getting you back on track. While it's an expensive exercise in getting those teeth looking fantastic, it is worth every dollar if your path to power necessitates a smile for the cameras every now and then. Smiling in politics is crucial as it reflects a sense of confidence and reassures people that everything is under control. So make sure those teeth don't let you down, as they did for former New Zealand PM Helen Clark.

Poor Helen Clark was the epitome of poor dentistry that displayed itself in all its glory every time she cracked a smile. Fortunately for her adoring fellow countrymen, she was a very serious lady and rarely had the need to smile. Helen Elizabeth Clark (1950–) was the thirty-seventh PM of New Zealand for three consecutive terms from 1999 to 2008 and the first elected female PM in New Zealand's history. Her official portrait, taken in 2005, has been touched up to brighten her smile, and the grey crooked teeth have been meticulously airbrushed many shades whiter than their natural grey appearance. Helen Clark obviously felt no need to spruce up her physical image for the media as she quite rightly considered matters of the state far more important than one's appearance. I'm not sure what

New Zealanders may have thought about their PM, but across the Tasman, Australians wondered whether New Zealand dentistry was falling behind the rest of the world whenever their cherished PM cracked one of those rare smiles.

Hair is an obvious feature that people particularly remember. The UK PM Boris Johnson deliberately ruffles his blond mop of hair every time he is seen in public as an attention-seeking ritual that signals he is different from your typical straight-laced politician. Long hair, ponytails, man-buns, dyed hair, and thickly lacquered manes like those of many Latin American leaders cannot be condoned for Western male politicians. Furthermore, unless you're planning to govern a Middle Eastern country, moustaches are ill-advised. After World War II, the toothbrush moustache fell from favour in the West because of its strong association with Hitler, earning it the nickname 'Hitler moustache'. The despot dictator Saddam Hussein, who ruled Iraq with terror and repression until he was deposed by the Americans in 2003, was typical of the mustachio-wearing rulers who could have easily shared the same family genes as the other mustachio dictator, Joseph Stalin, whom we met in Chapter 1. Physically, Saddam's appearance was that of a strong, handsome, masculine figure, which reinforced his iron grip on a fractious nation that was only fully recognised when the American-led coalition forces lost control of law and order after Saddam was toppled from power. We will meet him again later.

People like their leaders to be nicely groomed and conservatively dressed. Multiple earrings, other facial piercings, and visible tattoos on any politician are no-go zones as their appearance may scare off a largely conservative voting public. A shrewd political leader must dress the part of a smart and stylish individual who looks ready to do business. It is impossible to underestimate the power of a well-groomed individual who exudes confidence from their appearance alone. To play the part, you must look the part. The casual look with the open-neck shirt in parliament does not go down well with the party machine or the voting public. However, there are exceptions when it comes to sartorial choices that are driven by propaganda.

Russian president Vladimir Putin had no problem showing off his physical strength and physique with his shirtless horse-riding prowess or his karate skills on his hapless opponents, wearing the black-belt karate attire in front of the cameras. Former Australian PM Tony Abbott, who was a keen athlete, had no qualms about emerging from the Bondi surf beach in front of the assembled press photographers in his tight budgie smugglers (Australian slang for a vanishingly small bathing costume). On another front, any discerning politician who really cares about his appearance would steer clear of the APEC conferences when all the world leaders line up for a family group photo dressed in silly shirts mandated by tradition and supplied by the host nation. Over the years, world leaders have worn barongs in the Philippines, hanboks in South Korea, raincoats in Australia, ponchos in Chile, and leather jackets in Canada. Politicians wearing silly hats can sometimes court disaster, especially if the hat appears awkward, too large, or too small or is inadvertently worn backward. In some cases, the press can have a field day at the expense of the politician looking ridiculous, with hair nets taking the top prize for hilarity, especially when visiting clean rooms in factories or biological facilities.

A politician's dress sense must reflect their high position, so it is wise to avoid brightly coloured suits and Homer Simpson ties if you want the public to take you seriously. The 1970s were a time where fashion hit rock bottom, which was no better epitomised than the garish dress style of Australia's immigration minister under the Whitlam Labour government, Al Grassby (1972–1975). As the father of multiculturalism in Australia, Grassby also gained wide attention for his flamboyant dress sense – his colourful ties and brightly coloured suits that set him apart from the unwritten dress code for politicians of sombre dark suits and plain ties. It is no wonder Michael Portillo, the ex-British MP, quit politics altogether and now travels the railways of the world in his brightly coloured shirts, trousers, and jackets that celebrate his liberation from the drab dress code of Westminster.

Fortunately, Australian politics has since been spared of such tasteless attire, and in more recent times, Paul Keating has shown what a smart and snappy dress sense can do for your career. As Australia's twenty-fourth PM, the Right Honourable Paul Keating (1944–) was known as the man with the reptilian tongue and a snappy dress sense. His flair for tailor-made European-style suits were espoused by his predilection for French antique clocks, which was counter to his working-class roots and cantankerous parliamentary style. As federal treasurer in the Hawke Labour government from 1983 to 1991, Keating was behind the various microeconomic reforms and pursued economic policies and restructuring, such as floating the Australian dollar in 1983. After his toppling Bob Hawke in a leadership spill in 1991, most commentators believed that the 1993 federal election was 'unwinnable' as the Labour government had been at the helm for ten years and the pace of economic recovery from the early 1990s recession was sluggish. However, Keating succeeded in winning back the electorate with a strong campaign attacking the opposition's 'fightback' and a determined plan to reduce unemployment. Keating led Labour to an unforeseen election victory despite presiding over a recession that he publicly declared that Australia had to have. Whether his immaculate dress sense and style made a difference to his 'unwinnable' election victory will never be known.

Female political leaders are more likely to be publicly scrutinised by their general appearance because their hair, dress, and make-up are invariably more demanding than those of their male counterparts. They must deal with a significantly wider choice of wardrobe than the simple dark business suits that their male colleagues can get away with. Power suits are certainly welcomed, but serious female politicians avoid flaunting physical assets that may detract from their political endeavours. While subtle make-up is welcomed, heavy eyeliners and glossy lipsticks are distracting as people like to see politicians with natural looks that suggest probity. In recent times, the PMs of the UK (Theresa May, 2016–2019) and Australia (Julia Gillard, 2010–2013) were ladies with stylish appearances that nicely reflected their positions of high office. The Right Honourable Julia Gillard carried a simple but stylish coiffure that suited her position and complemented her appearance very well. The prize for the archetype 'best-dressed woman in Australian political history', however, goes to Julie Bishop, the minister for foreign affairs (2013–2018), who always looked immaculate with a great sense of style and taste in clothes, hair, jewellery, and make-up that reflected the seriousness of her position.

While we are on the topic of gender, history has largely excluded women from political power even though there have been a few notable exceptions like Cleopatra, Catherine the Great, and Queen Victoria. Universal female suffrage has only been a relatively recent phenomenon and largely introduced in most countries during the twentieth century. Likewise, the corridors of power have been the exclusive domain of men, with women parliamentarians gradually making their appearance in the early decades of the last century. Today women hold about a quarter of the parliamentary seats around the world, including the U.S. House of Representatives. Female rulers have been even less forthcoming, with the UK voting in their first female PM in 1979 and Australia in 2010, and the

United States is yet to have a female president, although Kamala Harris has made it to the U.S. vice presidency.

So how do women differ from men when it comes to politics? We know for a fact that men and women are simply good at different things. Women are generally more resistant to hunger, disease, and fatigue, while men are generally more ambitious and competitive. Women tend to be better at reading social signals and perform better in interactive and social settings. Women are often intent on formulating the problem when discussing something, while men are often wanting to fix things too early in the discussion. Men are expected to be assertive and women communal. Unfortunately, even modern society still forms stereotypical views of strong women in positions of authority and power. For instance, when women speak up or are assertive, they are judged as aggressive. When a woman tries to lead, she is judged as being bossy, and when she puts forth an idea, she is ignored until the same idea is repeated by a male colleague who adopts it as his own. Women who are assertive, dominant, and independent face the most harassment, especially in male-dominated organisations. A high-achieving woman inflicts greater feelings of inferiority in both other women and men. The best feminine traits are patience, resilience, and flexibility. The feminine style is more about maintaining group spirit and keeping relationships smoothed out, with fewer differences amongst individuals. Men overestimate their abilities and display confidence in their skills and place emphasis on results, however they are achieved. The feminine spirit emphasises cooperation over hierarchy. Therefore, women bring a very different style of leadership to the political sphere.

When the time comes where women make up 50 per cent or more of the political talent, I'm sure the world will be a much more peaceful and accommodating place than what it currently is today. While women must work hard to get a foot in the political door, feminine charm and appearance can certainly work in their favour. A political leader's appearance is a public reflection of their standing in society, and they are expected to look the part. Any attempt to develop your own unique style of dress and appearance will only succeed if it falls within acceptable limits because the public can only tolerate a narrow range of conservative styles of dress and grooming. Public expectation is what politicians need to fulfil, and a clean, smart, and attractive appearance goes hand in hand with success. If you want to impress, concentrate on your dress.

While poor grooming may be an initial setback for some, there are plenty of examples of ordinary leaders with ordinary appearances who have done extremely well in the political arena. Take the example of the German chancellor Angela Merkel, who may not have dazzled the world with her ordinary appearance, but she sure left a lasting legacy as a truly effective and well-respected world leader. While there are plenty of examples of very ordinary-looking political leaders who have been extremely successful in politics, you need everything in your favour to attract that initial positive attention you require to catapult you into the political arena. Ordinary people do eventually succeed, but their paths to glory may not be as smooth and as rapid as someone with stylish good looks, like Canada's PM Justin Trudeau, that ooze confidence. Being attractive may get you a foot in the door, but once you're in, the value of your appearance diminishes significantly if you cannot properly navigate the corridors of power. Appearance is only the first of many steps that you require to reach the top of the political pyramid.

***

On the last day of summer in 1997, a speeding black Mercedes was making its way through the narrow tunnels below the streets of Paris when it lost control and slammed into concrete pillars. In pursuit were photojournalists on motorbikes trying to capture photos of the passengers in the back seat. The world was stunned, and the media went into a frenzy when the world's most recognisable princess was pronounced dead.

The media rely on drama and negative news to grab your attention, which explains why we are more likely to be exposed to negative stories. Negative stories are more dramatic than positive ones, so journalists focus on negative news such as wars, natural disasters, famines, corruption, and political mistakes, which help to mentally invigorate the mind of the viewer or reader who is otherwise living a normal, boring life. The media's fondness for bad news can be blamed on a cynical chase for eyeballs and clicks because bad news makes a stronger impact than good news. Princess Diana's untimely death was a tragedy that galvanised the world's media so much that Mother Teresa's death on the same day was barely mentioned. When things get better, we don't often hear about it as good news is rarely reported. Social media platforms know what makes you click, what grabs your attention most, so they dish up more sensational clickbait to maintain your attention for the sake of lucrative personalised advertising. After all, 'boring' and 'nice' do not sell. It is often the fear instinct that most strongly influences the media's choice of stories that they present to the consumer. We can cynically say that fears that once kept our ancestors alive today help keep journalists employed. While the media portray the world as a much scarier place than what it really is, the paradox is that the world today is the safest it has been in all of human history. If we pay more attention to the facts, we will see that the world is not as bad as the media make it out to be.

According to Churchill, the media often exercise power without responsibility. Soft power is the ability to influence others without using force, which is often in the hands of those who control the message. So if journalists or opinion writers deliberately choose ignorance and intellectual laziness, then the wrong message is conveyed to the masses. Journalists prefer anecdotes over data since anecdotes are harder to discredit and provide an immediate hook for the reader. Most people enjoy believing stories propagated by journalists and often do not care about their factuality. A contagious story is one that quickly grabs the attention of and makes an impression on another person, regardless of whether it is true or not. Often an illusion spreads faster than the fact that disproves it. In other words, the person in control of the media megaphone may completely ignore the evidence as there are no ethical constraints when it comes to freedom of speech. Not surprisingly, policy is influenced more by media sentiment than by independent expert opinion, which puts most politicians on the back foot when it comes to policy decisions. In noisy public arenas, strident voices dominate debates and are heard most because they are the loudest, and the media reward people who shout into their megaphones.

The response of the political system is guided by the intensity of public sentiment, which is fuelled by the exaggeration of minor threats by the media, who compete for attention-grabbing headlines. In political circles, it is well established that you never allow a crisis to go to waste. Road trauma and domestic violence are much greater risks than terrorism, yet governments pour more resources into terrorism because policymakers must protect the public from fear that is fuelled by the media, regardless of whether it is rational or not. While on the surface, we think of the media as the conduit for information, deep down, what the media are really looking for is an entertaining news story that people will read or switch to. News editors look to fill their morning papers or evening news broadcasts with entertaining stories that seize the attention of the average reader or television viewer or, increasingly, the social media aficionado.

It is little wonder that reality TV and trashy soap operas are so popular, simply because their entertainment value does not require any deep and meaningful thought process.

By and large, the public only see and hear about their leader through the radio, television, social media, and, less so, newspapers. It is largely from the perspective of the reporters and their editors that a picture of political leaders is built up in the minds of the voting public. A hostile media can undermine the power and influence of political leaders because in a free society, the media are free to report what they like, and political leaders are not spared from criticism. Media do not like stiff, uneasy political figures who appear clumsy or awkward during interviews or in front of cameras. Because there is a natural tendency for people to find uncertainty disturbing, the media gravitate to confident political figures who tell succinct, simple, clear stories that grab and hold audiences.

In the normal course of political life, politicians seek and nurture popularity through positive speeches that embellish their achievements. Even when there is only negative news, politicians often avoid telling people things that provoke a negative response. If there is a choice between getting a round of applause for what people want to hear and a round of jeers and boos for telling them the truth, then it is not very difficult to see how a round of applause is what all politicians strive for. Media are unlikely to gravitate to super-intelligent politicians who have a dry and long-winded delivery of the facts. What they look for are entertaining larrikins who offer crisp, concise sound bites for the evening news. The more outrageous the comments are, the more likely they'll appear on the evening news and go viral on social media. Therefore, to court the media, politicians need to present their stories in an entertaining sound bite. For example, an entertaining sound bite from a Greens senator, who has trivial political powers, is more likely to hit the news headlines than a long-winded monologue from the nation's foreign minister, who has more political clout in the grand scheme of things.

Serious political shows attract only the hardcore political buffs. As an aspiring political leader, if you want to extend your reach to 'Main Street', feature articles about your pets or favourite recipes in lifestyle magazines or tabloid newspapers may do the trick. Just steer away from controversial subjects like assisted suicide and abortion and stick to popular topics like sports, cooking, and your favourite pastimes. The average man on the street wants to know if the person leading the country actually has a real life outside of politics. In other words, is the PM a person who can connect with the public at large so that they understand what the ordinary man on the street feels? A prudent leader should occasionally attend popular talk shows in the category of light entertainment as political minders see it as a nice publicity stunt to get political leaders better acquainted with their politically indifferent voters who watch these programmes. This is where the media can create an engaging profile of a political leader that opens a window to the public at large through which ordinary people can see their leader as a person like themselves. All it takes is to cultivate a cosy relationship with the media barons and their top journalists and editors to make sure that media reports are positive and stay positive.

How we manage and assess risk is one of the most important aspects of our characters and how we live. Journalists take refuge in their vocation by watching and reporting without taking risks, so they are at liberty to prod, ask, and provoke politicians for responses that are designed to elicit maximum emotional responses that could do them a lot of damage and make the journalist a hero. There is nothing worse than a toxic relationship between politicians and the media. Leaders should avoid public declarations of war with the media and never openly criticise media outlets, even if they are delivering biased reporting. That is why seasoned politicians get to know all the main journalists and political reporters at a personal level and perhaps hold an informal function every once in a while for them. Remember – the media are the window through which the public at large see their politicians at work. Any animosity between politicians and the media will quickly tarnish or destroy the politician's image in the public eye.

The media are clever at manipulating the truth, so politicians must be careful about how they react to journalist questions designed to provoke awkward or damaging responses. Media personalities love to interview politicians live in their own studios as they are fully aware that the politician is out of their own comfort zone amongst the bright studio lights. What is even worse is the hostile studio audience handpicked by TV producers who love an entertaining stoush at the expense of the politician. Personal one-on-one media interviews with hostile reporters should be avoided as far as possible as their intention is to provoke the politician by asking questions that will trigger adverse or emotional responses that make the politician look bad. Even for an experienced politician, it is hard to beat a seasoned reporter or media host who has strong views one way or the other, particularly if you're trying to spruik a policy that the media host obviously does not like.

A clever media adviser should easily be able to identify and court friendly media outlets and reporters to cover most interviews and events. Although it is hard to stop hostile reporters from gate-crashing your media appearances, a confident and experienced politician should be able to neutralise them by focusing on giving detailed answers to questions from friendly media and short, sharp responses to those less-than-friendly questions. To prepare for a media encounter, it is imperative that you lean on your cabinet and media advisers to make sure you are fully briefed with all the facts and figures by trying to second-guess the most obvious questions that reporters will ask you. Employing an experienced former political reporter as part of your media advisory staff is a must. When confronted with tricky questioning, it's best to say the matter needs to be properly discussed with your cabinet colleagues/minister responsible before you can make any further comment. Try not to be led up the garden path by clever reporters who are trying to extract an answer by cajoling you with responses like 'But you haven't answered my question'.

The incentives for political leaders are skewed to issues that are likely to attract plenty of media coverage, such as the opening of a sensational new sports stadium or a world-class museum of contemporary art. Opening a new aged care facility or refurbished country hospital may be a highlight for the local community but is not a riveting news story, and so leaders should seriously consider sending deputies to such events when pressed for time. Busy leaders should stick to big news events where the media take a keen interest and are likely to broadcast the event as a top item news story. While there is much kudos to be gained by politicians who woo the company of celebrities, sports stars, national heroes, and industry leaders, it is also imperative for political leaders to be seen chatting freely amongst the ordinary people and be seen doing ordinary things like walking their dog. Courting the media is part and parcel of political life and needs to be carefully cultivated so that a positive spin is placed on the leadership. Media advisors and 'spin doctors' can only do so much in improving a political leader's media performance.

The former Victorian premier, John Brumby, was a natural media player who was comfortable in front of the cameras and showed it too. Manipulating the media, like the late Princess Diana did during her short but eventful life, requires a clever and cunning approach. Diana used intermediaries to tip off reporters to events that, on the surface, appeared private but, in fact, were deliberately staged. In the end, it didn't matter that Diana was manipulating the media because the media were happy to oblige since her image was her trademark that sold countless newspapers and magazines as well as generated enormous ratings for TV news broadcasts worldwide.

Diana, Princess of Wales (Diana Frances née Spencer; 1961–1997), was born into an old, aristocratic English family with royal ancestry and became the first wife of Charles, Prince of Wales, whom she married on 29 July 1981 at St Paul's Cathedral in London. From the announcement of her engagement to the Prince of Wales, Diana became an international personality of the late twentieth century and remained the focus of worldwide media scrutiny before, during, and after her marriage to Prince Charles, which ended in divorce on 28 August 1996, but that wasn't the end of Diana. The media just couldn't get enough of her, and she was happy to oblige as the public face of dozens of charities and causes, most prominently the International Campaign to Ban Landmines, which focused on the injuries that mines create, often to children, long after a conflict is over.

Her difficult marriage to Prince Charles, which fuelled her depression, made her restless, spiteful, and manipulative. She became obsessed with her public image, which brought her power as a media-savvy neurotic and borderline personality disorder out for revenge. Her ultimate demise came with an ill-conceived romantic relationship with Dodi Fayed that was meant to anger the royal Family but ended with her tragic death in a Parisian tunnel at summer's end in 1997. The week of mourning and funeral brought one last crisis to the British royal family, who had to finally concede that Diana was loved by all. Her untimely death, it seems, was her ultimate revenge against the House of Windsor, who were brought out of hiding to face the hostile public, who felt that some of the blame should rest with the royal family, who shunned her in her final years. During the sixteen years she had graced the world stage, her iconic presence shone brightly, and she was often described as the world's most photographed woman. From her engagement to the Prince of Wales in 1981 until her untimely and tragic death in 1997, Diana was noted for her style, personality, and high-profile charity work, which brought with it a compassionate feel. Diana was an exceptional media manipulator, which brought her the love and respect she craved from the public at large, something that was missing from the British royal establishment.

It is well recognised that the most powerful people in the country are, in fact, the media barons, who are constantly courted by PMs and presidents the world over. Politicians clearly agree that media owners are people who can make or break their careers and often go out of their way to keep on friendly terms. Dinner with Rupert Murdoch, the ubiquitous media chief, is always on the must-do list of priorities for all Australian and British PMs who visit the United States. Snubbing old Rupert while you're in the neighbourhood is akin to setting fire to your home as Rupert is all too pleased to provide the fuel. For those who find the business of greasing up to others rather disconcerting, why not buy some media outlets to help promote your magnificent image? If you're blessed with deep pockets – like the Italian master of manipulation, Silvio Berlusconi – why not buy all the media outlets and get yourself elected so that you can change the laws to suit your tastes and lifestyle?

Silvio Berlusconi (1936–) was the third longest serving PM of Italy, after Benito Mussolini and Giovanni Giolitti. He was PM on three separate occasions: from 1994 to 1995, from 2001 to 2006, and from 2008 to 2011. Interestingly, Silvio Berlusconi has an extensive record of criminal allegations, including corruption and bribery of police officers and judges, Mafia collusion, false accounting, and tax fraud, just to name a few. While he has been tried in Italian courts on numerous occasions, accusations were dropped by the judiciary because of laws passed by Berlusconi's parliamentary majority – pretty good effort for a leading politician who is meant to serve the public but has used his political powers to bolster his defences against criminal convictions.

Despite his numerous run-ins with the law, Berlusconi proudly portrays himself as the man who gave Italians a more fair and efficient judicial system. Former prosecutors and magistrates who have attempted to pin guilt on the PM later joined the parliamentary opposition, while some of his own attorneys who defended him have also become members of parliament – quite a circus, no doubt – and if you think changing the laws to protect yourself from prosecution sounds bizarre, Berlusconi also controlled 90 per cent of the Italian national media, which severely limits freedom of expression and threatens news diversity in what is supposed to be a free and democratic nation.

While internal media have been effectively gagged by Berlusconi's extensive control over the media, international newsprint like the *Economist* had no fear in claiming the Italian PM is corrupt and self-serving. His many public sexual indiscretions, while highly scandalous, appear to have done little damage to his power base, even though his reputation both nationally and internationally was severely tarnished. So even in a modern free and democratic society, if you own the media and you make the rules, there is nothing that can possibly stand in your way.

Power and influence can only be maintained by a symbiotic relationship between politicians and the media, so you ignore the media at your peril. The media need news stories, and the politicians need exposure, so a clever politician should willingly feed stories to the media. Never let the media chase you for stories. Be proactive and engage the media on a regular basis so that you can carefully control what gets out to the media. If you fail to satisfy the media's insatiable appetite for political news, then the media will often invent their own stories that may not be to your liking. A seasoned politician appreciates the power of the media by respecting their need to report news. So it pays to court the media like you court a lover, but just make sure you don't jilt them because you may come out looking second best.

CHAPTER 3

Humility and the Human Touch

The ancient Greek philosopher Plato said, 'The best people for positions of power and authority are those who do not seek it because those who do are most likely to be corrupted by the experience.' The rise to positions of power often begins with the friendliest and most empathetic people who are modest and kind-hearted to begin with. Once in power, these same people may become more impulsive, self-centred, reckless, arrogant, and rude. Confidence can easily tip over into overconfidence, which becomes a liability. Ignorance goes hand in hand with overconfidence because there are none so blind as those who will not see. True ignorance is not the absence of knowledge but rather the refusal to acquire it, so the very stupid and the powerful have one thing in common: they don't alter their views to fit the facts; rather, they alter the facts to fit their views.

In whatever field you choose to follow, concentrate on maintaining a high sense of purpose, and success will flow naturally to you. The most successful people are those who can effectively understand, synthesise, and communicate information and ideas. Good leadership requires a good dose of humility and sacrifice; otherwise, reckless abandon, obstinacy, and arrogance may become your downfall. Humility is a useful asset and must be cultivated by those starting out on their journey to political power because Western politicians are not elected to rule over their people but to serve them as their faithful representative. Leaders who rule by means of arrogance rather than humility only destroy their popularity and create animosity with their own colleagues. Humility is an important key you can use to open the doors of power because modesty fuels respect and respect is what you need to go places. Being polite and friendly can make people around you pliable and obliging. Few people can warm to egotistical, supercilious individuals who take pleasure in their own self-importance. These people show little interest in matters beyond themselves. They embellish stories and would make fantastic fiction writers if they stopped talking and took up pen and paper instead. The famous U.S. writer Ernest Hemingway did just that and won worldwide acclaim for his books, which became literary classics. Had he not been a writer, his tales of bravery would have fallen on deaf ears as people clearly suspected that his personal accounts of heroism during both world wars were highly exaggerated.

Anyone who wants to change the world should be humble. Small incremental steps are the only safe path forward. It pays to recognise your limits and the possibility of failure, consider uncertainty, remain open to new information, recognise the potential to grow from errors, and actively question everything. A humble approach to party matters often identifies you as a potential leader who is most likely to toe the party line. Openly ambitious, aggressive, and arrogant party members are considered a liability for the party, and these members are often overlooked by the powerbrokers who see a quiet, modest, and affable person with respectable intelligence as the ideal leader. In a leadership tussle, you need the support of lots of influential people so you avoid conflicts that may harm your supporter base. Boisterous individuals leave nothing to the imagination and bury themselves in foolhardy conversation, which can be a great source of irritation to those around them. Folks who speak in deliberate and restrained ways become a fascinating focus of attention, especially if their carefully considered statements reflect an intelligent and thoughtful individual. A thoughtful response is always better than a confident boast. You need to demonstrate flashes of brilliance in front of your colleagues but never openly push your own barrow. People are apt to listen to a colleague's endorsement of you as opposed to paying any attention to activities that reek of self-promotion. It is perhaps best to have others lobby on your behalf as people tend to respect other people's opinions of you. After all, the opinions that matter most come from those we trust.

We learn more from failure than success because it is loss that teaches us the worth of things. In other words, you cannot understand the value of something until it is gone. From adversity comes greatness because it makes you even more determined. The tragic loss of his young family in the 1970s and his adult son a few years back made U.S. president Joe Biden more stoic and resilient than he would otherwise have been. Loss makes you appreciate the important things in life, like family and friendships that you may perhaps overlook in your quest for glory. Leadership can be a humbling experience as well as overwhelming if you don't have the right support behind you. That is why family and friendships are fundamental to your success. Being humble, however, is not enough. You also need to be quietly ambitious, confidently astute, and brilliantly clever but with a restrained ego and a veiled determination that you can rely on to get you through tough times. There is no more famous a person than Gandhi, who was the epitome of humility and yet managed to mobilise a nation and leave a legacy that still reverberates today.

Mohandas Karamchand Gandhi (1869–1948) was a preeminent political and ideological leader of India who pioneered non-violent mass civil resistance to tyranny during the Indian independence movement that inspired other movements for civil rights and freedom across the globe. His philosophy and leadership helped India gain independence, and he is officially honoured in India as the 'Father of the Nation'. The life of Gandhi, as an expatriate lawyer in South Africa in the early 1900s, was shaped by the discrimination, prejudice, and racism directed at Indians, and this was a turning point which kindled his social activism to fight social injustice. Gandhi's personal experiences with discrimination brought into question his place in society and his people's standing in the British Empire, but it was in South Africa where Gandhi first employed civil disobedience during the struggle for civil rights for the resident Indian community.

He returned to India in 1915, where an excessive land tax and discrimination against peasants, farmers, and urban labourers prompted him to stage organised protests. Gandhi then went on to lead nationwide campaigns to ease poverty, end untouchability, increase economic self-reliance, build religious and ethnic amity, and expand women's rights. After assuming leadership of the Indian National Congress in 1921, he began the long process to achieve the independence of India from British domination. It was during the intense Nazi bombardment of British cities and towns that Gandhi launched the Quit India Movement in 1942, demanding immediate independence for India from British rule, as a response to Britain's call to arms from their Indian subjects. For his efforts,

Gandhi was again jailed by the authorities – a pattern that was all too common throughout his life.

Gandhi employed non-cooperation and peaceful resistance as his arsenal in the struggle against British rule, believing that violence was evil and could not be justified. The principle of non-violence has a long history in Christian, Jewish, and Hindu religious thought, but Gandhi was the first to apply it in the political field on a large scale. Civil disobedience and non-cooperation as practised under satyagraha was a means to secure the cooperation of the opponent with truth and justice or moral power as opposed to physical power. As the consummate practitioner of humility, Gandhi believed that a person involved in public service should lead a simple life. He gave up wearing Western-style clothing, which he associated with wealth and success, and renounced the Western lifestyle he had led in South Africa. Gandhi wore the traditional Indian *dhoti* and shawl and lived modestly in a self-sufficient residential community. Gandhi dressed to be accepted by the poorest of India, advocating the practice of weaving one's own clothes from the thread they themselves spun on a charkha, a spinning device which was later incorporated into the flag of the Indian National Congress. He undertook long fasts as a means of both social protest and self-purification. The practices of giving up unnecessary expenditure, returning gifts bestowed on him by grateful communities, and washing his own clothes were part of Gandhi's efforts to embrace a simple lifestyle devoid of any luxuries.

Gandhi proved that a simple life of quiet determination rather than a turgid and pretentious style of confrontation can have powerful consequences that can rally a nation. Gandhi's legacy had far-reaching effects on the anti-apartheid activities in South Africa and the civil rights movement in the United States. Leaders such as Martin Luther King Jr. and Nelson Mandela were inspired by the writings of Gandhi, whose influence helped shape their own non-violent struggles against racial discrimination. One of these iconic personalities of the twentieth century spent over a quarter century behind bars fighting for a just cause.

Nelson Rolihlahla Roandela (1918–2013) was South Africa's first president to be elected in a fully representative democratic election. His road to power was long and difficult, with his having spent twenty-seven years in prison after he was arrested in 1962 and convicted of sabotage and other charges as an anti-apartheid activist. Following his release from prison on 11 February 1990, Mandela led his party to multi-racial democratic elections that saw him ascend to the presidency of South Africa in 1994. For someone who had spent twenty-seven years behind bars, he was very forgiving and frequently gave priority to reconciliation during his term as president. Mandela's approach and those of succeeding generations of anti-apartheid activists in South Africa were greatly influenced Mahatma Gandhi's satyagraha or non-violent resistance.

The initial commitment to non-violent resistance was short-lived, and following years of increasing repression and violence from the state, Mandela was convinced that non-violent protest against apartheid had not and could not achieve any progress, and the move to armed struggle was a last resort. As leader of the armed wing of the African National Congress (ANC), he raised funds from abroad and immediately commenced sabotage campaigns against military and government targets. A bombing campaign to end apartheid led by Mandela was to start in December 1961 to blast the symbolic places of apartheid, like pass offices and native magistrates' courts, and other government offices linked to the repression of black people. With a tip-off from the U.S. Central Intelligence Agency (CIA), security police apprehended Mandela in August 1962 after he was on the run for seventeen months.

During his trial in April 1964 at the Pretoria Supreme Court, Mandela laid out his defence in the ANC's use of violence as a tactic and said, 'During my lifetime, I have dedicated myself to the struggle of the African people. I have fought against white domination, and I have fought against black domination. I have cherished the ideal of a democratic and free society in which all persons live together in harmony and with equal opportunities. It is an ideal which I hope to live for and to achieve. But if needs be, it is an ideal for which I am prepared to die.' Mandela was found guilty and was sentenced to life imprisonment in 1964.

Mandela was imprisoned on Robben Island, and while he was in jail, his reputation as the most significant black leader in South Africa grew, while local and international pressure intensified on the South African government to release him. In February 1985, Pres P. W. Botha offered Mandela his freedom, but Mandela spurned the offer, releasing a statement via his daughter Zindzi, saying, 'What freedom am I being offered while the organisation of the people remains banned?' In 1989, President Botha suffered a stroke and was replaced as president by Frederik Willem de Klerk, who promptly reversed the ban on the ANC and other anti-apartheid organisations and announced that Mandela would be released from the Victor Verster Prison in Paarl on 11 February 1990. The release became an international media event and was broadcast live to cheering millions all over the world.

Following his release, Mandela quickly returned to the leadership of the ANC after the ban was lifted when he was elected president at its first national conference in 1991. Between 1990 and 1994, Mandela focused his attention on bringing peace to the black majority and giving them the right to vote in national elections. Mandela's leadership, through the negotiations and good relationship with Pres F. W. de Klerk, was recognised when they were jointly awarded the Nobel Peace Prize in 1993, despite the violence that threatened to stall talks and destabilise the negotiation process. The negotiators were eventually galvanised into action and agreed that democratic elections should take place on 27 April 1994. In South Africa's first multi-racial elections, held on 27 April 1994, the ANC won 62 per cent of the votes in the election, and Mandela was inaugurated as the country's first black president on 10 May 1994 and became the oldest elected president of South Africa when he took office at the age of seventy-five. As president, Mandela presided over the demise of minority rule and apartheid, gaining international admiration for his advocacy of national reconciliation. He declined a second term and retired in 1999 and was succeeded by Thabo Mbeki. Following his retirement in 1999, the UN adopted 18 July as an annual international day called Mandela Day, commemorating the sixty-seven years that Nelson Mandela gave to the struggle for social justice.

As we have seen, some of the greatest figures of the twentieth century were the humblest leaders who appreciated that people power was much stronger than any individual. The pursuit of truth and honesty was the very basis of humility which provided the strength for these leaders to follow their vision for a just society where equality could be found in opportunity. A clear vision is the compass that turns dreams into reality. Hardships are faced by many leaders in their quest for the top job, but it takes a very special leader, like Mandela, to forgive those who block their path. Perhaps the greatest demonstration of strength is the ability to turn the other cheek, like Gandhi and Mandela so effectively proved. It shows courage and determination and makes your opponents appear like thugs not fit to rule.

Humility is a permeable filter that absorbs life's experiences and converts it to knowledge and wisdom. All politicians, no matter how hard it may be, require a certain dose of intellectual humility; otherwise, it is impossible for them to learn if they can't admit that they might be wrong. Pride and arrogance curtail our ability to learn, to adapt, to be flexible, and to build relationships. Arrogance leaves us blind to our weaknesses. You will do better when you take on board a criticism at an early stage of your political career. We often make the mistake of spending an enormous amount of time and energy trying to boost our self-esteem and confidence when in fact, we should accept the reality that we cannot know it all. These are key considerations because when politicians are under threat, mistakes are made when they take a single-minded, inflexible approach to what is often a multifaceted problem. Respect must be earned, affection must be won, and authority must be used sparingly if it is to be effective. Humility and mutual respect are two of the sustainable values that generate trust, social bonds, and hope for a better outcome. Humility also attracts supporters, and supporters are what you need in your quest for political power.

Nothing is a more powerful motivator than to know that you are making a difference in the world or to other people's lives, and that's what politics does. Humanism focuses on the well-being of individual men, women, and children rather than the glory of the tribe, race, religion, or nation. Modern political power is not innate but granted based on ability, knowledge, persuasion, and force of personality. So it takes a special person with the right combination of these talents to succeed in the rough-and-tumble world of politics. Politics can be a nasty business, particularly for those who lack the essential skills required to cultivate interpersonal relationships. People with self-esteem do not depend on others for attention and recognition. If you lack self-esteem, you will always be worried about what others think of you. People who are insecure or lack confidence are always comparing themselves to others. Our desire for approval from those around us determines our moral compass, especially when we experience approval or disapproval from others. Social feedback that we give and receive influences how we behave and how others behave in response to our reactions. Those who are emotionally dependent are influenced by others' opinions of them, which shapes their sense of worth and security. Being around people stirs up our insecurities and anxieties as to how others perceive us. Aspiring politicians need to rise above all this by accepting that there are many things you cannot control. Therefore, you need to steer clear of anger and anxiety over things you can't control because angry people usually end up looking foolish, for their response seems blown out of proportion to what occasioned it.

The relative strength of someone's character is gauged on how well they handle adversity. Difficult experiences and circumstances can be the crucibles that forge strong characters that can inspire others. We see the world through a lens we call attitude. Our attitude determines much of what happens to us in life. We can alter our lives by altering our attitudes, and a positive attitude will help us learn from adversity and create opportunities out of nothing. Confidence is attitude linked to positive thinking. When negative people seek advice for a particular problem or symptom, they find dozens of reasons why the advice given won't work for them. Therefore, the best way to deal with negative people is to heartily agree with their rebellion and tell them to keep doing what they're doing, which now means they are following your advice, which, of course, they do not want to do. Those who find it difficult to connect with the common man or woman on the street will find it impossible to succeed in politics, no matter how clever and intelligent they may be. It seems that super-intelligent individuals sometimes lack the capacity for common sense and social sensitivity, where they fail to recognise and respond to the needs and expectations of the common man on the street. So a personable politician with a positive attitude is a must.

People are generally cynical of all politicians, so the onus is on the politician to prove that they care about family, society, and community. Knowing where you came from and how you came to be is an important part of your identity. Personal identity is meaningless without the context of the people you mix with because social isolation diminishes our very sense of who we are. If you want to form strong bonds with people, do not judge them but simply accept them as they are. Take note of temperaments and characters and adapt yourself to that of each person you meet. To figure out who people really are, you can't merely go by what they say. It is best to observe their behaviour. Know how to be all things to all men by being a liberal amongst liberals and a saint amongst saints.

Influence over other people does not work if they feel in any way that they are being coerced or manipulated. If you want to influence people's thoughts and opinions, plant the seed of an idea in a bland, non-coercive way so they feel it is their own idea. If you want to build a relationship, begin by disagreeing on a subject; then allow them to correct you and then slowly come round to seeing their point of view. Adopting a caring attitude by sharing the grief, sorrow, and burden of the forgotten people who struggle with the necessities of life is a good way to connect with people. However, it is better to be compassionate than empathetic to someone in need because empathy paralyses you, but compassion motivates you to act. The ability to understand the mood of the common man on the street is essential, and the need to target the disadvantaged with effective policies is paramount. The political process must ensure that the bottom dwellers of society are not ignored as their hapless plight can split the very fabric of social order and may result in civil unrest.

Communities can only thrive where there are ample employment opportunities because an economically prosperous community is what politicians need to hold onto their seats, and a thriving community needs to appreciate all the hard work their local political representative has put into making it a success. The key is to convey positive messages that clearly show who is responsible for the prosperity the community enjoys, and that requires a riveting public speech that details your achievements. The best speeches are masterpieces of visualisation, and a vision for a brighter future will inspire support for your policies. It takes the power of storytelling to engage people's minds, so avoid complex language where simpler language will do since easily pronounced words and names provoke a favourable response from your audience. Strive to make your message simple and memorable as you don't want to tax your audience with complexity that requires effort to understand. Pretentious language is taken as a sign of low credibility, so when making public speeches, politicians should immediately engage their audience with questions or statements that get straight to the heart of the issues of most concern to the community. Short, informative, and to-the-point speeches are imperative if people are to listen with any interest. If you want their attention, keep it simple and short. If you want change, throw in a crisis or two.

One of the most moving speeches in modern history was that given by U.S. president Ronald Reagan following the space shuttle *Challenger* disaster on 28 January 1986, where all seven astronauts were killed seventy-three seconds after lift-off. In a time of mourning, President Reagan left out politics and simply reflected on the mood of the nation following the shuttle disaster, with moving phrases that reflected the nation's loss. Reagan delivered a speech written by Peggy Noonan in which he said (quoting from the first and last lines of John Gillespie Magee Jr.'s 1941 poem 'High Flight'), '*The future doesn't belong to the fainthearted. It belongs to the brave . . . We will never forget them nor the last time we saw them this morning as they prepared for their journey and waved goodbye and "slipped the surly bonds of Earth" to "touch the face of God".'*

The Queensland floods of 2011 showed what a true leader needs to win the hearts and minds of the people. The premier of Queensland at the time, Anna Bligh, put on the most remarkable performance of any political leader of her time as she stood side by side with her emergency team leaders, in front of the nation's television cameras, explaining to her people the gravity of the situation and reassuring them that her government was doing everything possible to help. Her reassuring tone and conversational style delivery put everyone at ease. Before the floods, Anna Bligh's approval ratings were waning, but after the floods, they were restored to healthy levels.

If politicians want to be heard, they need to speak the people's language, a language all people can understand and immediately respond to in a positive way. Kevin Rudd's attempt to use Australian vernacular fell flat on its face because people know when you're pretending to be what you really are not. It's best to be candid with the people than beguiling as there is nothing worse than an exalted political leader with inflated views of themselves. The average citizen can often see through political smokescreens and is rarely impressed with haughty leaders who are seen as aloof and disconnected from the people.

The human touch is about leaders wanting to genuinely share in their people's joys and grief, their happiness and their sorrows, their triumphs and despairs. The antithesis of this are the despotic African leaders, like the infamous former Ugandan president Idi Amin, who pillage their country's riches and leave their subjects in abject poverty. The typical Ugandan citizen under Idi Amin's rule had no recourse for their hardships as their leader usurped his position of power and renounce his duty of care to his own citizens. In a true democracy, leaders arise from the people not by way of hereditary rights or despotic mechanisms but by meritocracy itself. A good leader can come from all walks of life. Ben Chifley, the Australian Labour PM of the late 1940s, was a train driver before he became leader of a nation. It's examples like Chifley that make the democratic process fair and equitable so that anyone with the skill and ability to lead has every opportunity to do so. This reassures the public that political leaders understand hardships and sorrow. One recent leader who understood the public mood better than most was Bob Hawke.

———

Robert James Lee 'Bob' Hawke (1929–2019) was the longest serving Labour PM in Australian history, winning four consecutive federal elections after coming to power at the 1983 federal election. Hawke was a leader with great authority who provided political guidance and consensus that helped drive economic reform. Hawke understood the public well, and he connected with people in a down-to-earth way. His daughter's public battle with drugs and his repeated teary interviews exposed the public to the human touch that Hawke was not afraid to show. Rather than a stoic front, Hawke showed the human side with tears and joy, something rarely seen in political leaders. Hawke was a consensus-driven politician who understood how to cultivate and nurture his popularity with the voting public, and this was cleverly adopted by Tony Blair, who led Labour to victory in the UK elections in 1998.

Few politicians feel comfortable about exposing their innermost feelings as it may show them to be weak or indecisive. Popular politicians are those who can demonstrate a strong bond with their people. There are countless activities that connect politicians with the ordinary man and woman on the street, and these should be promoted at every opportunity. Politicians need to feel comfortable around their people. There is a great photo of US president Nixon shaking a man's hand while looking away at his watch, giving the impression that the public were a nuisance and wasting his time. Politicians need to be amongst it all rather than be seen as bystanders or outsiders. You cannot have power without respect. Respect can be achieved and maintained in many ways, and one of the most effective ways is to be seen as one with the people.

Diana, the Princess of Wales, was adept at projecting the human touch when, during the height of AIDS/HIV hysteria in the mid-1980s, she was shown embracing AIDS patients at a time when the disease was considered highly contagious. Her message was simple yet powerful, and it underscored the importance of human dignity in the face of adversity. Diana became a people's princess as she reached out to all of society's dejected people whose suffering and pain were largely ignored. For all her faults, Diana had the knack for embracing those less fortunate who were concealed from the public consciousness. Unlike most politicians who visit the sick in hospitals, Diana would pull up a seat at the patient's bedside and position herself at the same eye level as the patient. Sadly, most politicians appear uneasy around the sick and, from a standing position, look down on the patients, which gives the impression of aloofness over their subject.

The human touch is something we are not all born with, and some politicians must work harder than others to comfortably connect with people, particularly strangers. In his time, the great scientist Albert Einstein was a remarkably amiable person whose popularity was fuelled by his simple approach to life. While he could never understand why there was so much public fascination about him that endured throughout his adult life, perhaps his simple pleasures such as playing his violin and sailing his small boat showed a very down-to-earth, human side to a genius who rivalled the great Isaac Newton in explaining the universe we live in. His immense popularity was exploited by his Jewish colleagues, who cajoled him into supporting charities and causes that eventually led to the establishment of the Jewish state of Israel. Einstein was a humble man with simple needs whose scientific revelations were understood by few people, and yet he was continually mobbed by strangers and reporters who were attracted by a paradox in the simplicity of a man who understood the complexities of the universe. In fact, Einstein was given the opportunity to become the first president of the newly created state of Israel, but he turned it down. Einstein's life was an incredible example of how a genius with a human touch could wield so much power and influence in world affairs. He was one of the signatories on the letter impressing on U.S. president Roosevelt to build the atomic bomb, and yet all he wanted in life was to be left alone to think about his grand unified theory of the universe and smoke his pipe. The human touch can be a very powerful tool, particularly for those seeking influence and power.

Political leaders can only understand the ordinary man and woman on the street if they themselves participate in the very activities that ordinary citizens participate in. An aloof ruler may be the norm in repressed societies, but aloofness does not sit well in a democratic society. Only by appearing relaxed when engaging ordinary people do politicians succeed in winning over the hearts and minds of the people. As we shall see later, the way that the public perceive you is crucially important.

Chapter 4

Know Your Friends and Enemies

Political power is never the property of an individual, for it belongs to a group. Therefore, individuals exercising power must continually nurture their links with the groups that fuel their power. Success sometimes means finding out who is important and hitching your wagon to them or at least forming alliances with them. Inside a major political party, you must ascertain who wields the power and get to know those party powerbrokers because only they can open the doors to leadership ambitions. In the game of politics, it is ludicrous to think that you can achieve your goals without the vital support of influential acquaintances, and they're not just any acquaintances. You need the backing of powerful people who wield plenty of influence in party matters to get you places. Without the crucial help of influential people to lubricate your path to glory, there will be immense disappointment and a great deal of soul searching.

In the world of who you know, the powerbrokers who drive the political machine are the most important individuals you need to cavort with. These are the faceless men and women in a political party who call the shots, and yet, paradoxically, they shun the limelight. We already discussed them in Chapter 1. Their power is based on their ability to influence all party matters. They command respect and have wide-ranging tentacles that spread their influence across many pies. Without their approval, you will never gain political power. Identifying the bigwigs in politics is easy. The hard part is trying to convince them that you are the best person to lead the party. Before they provide their crucial support, they must be satisfied that you will toe the party line and not do anything that would upset the harmony and unity of the party, which will be discussed in the next chapter. Political leaders are usually chosen for their ability to unite the party, so those with divisive personalities and capricious temperaments are side-lined in favour of collaborative and obliging individuals. Once in power, never forget who brought you to power and respect them because your position depends on their continued support.

When putting together your caucus or cabinet, make sure you choose people who are smart, secure in themselves, and loyal to you. Close friends aren't necessarily the best people to have on your team if they lack the aptitude and capacity to run a department or cover a portfolio that demands enormous skills and ability. Select people according to merit and avoid overly ambitious, insecure people who have a history of poor teamwork. What you don't need in your close circle of trusted associates are people with inflated egos, imprudent behaviour, and a beguiling manner that may easily upset the delicate balance and harmony of your cabinet. Probity and intelligence are essential qualities that you should look for when courting political allies, so avoid making pacts or promises with colleagues in exchange for their support if you feel they just don't have what it takes to assume responsibilities that should ideally go to more capable people.

The government serves the interest of those who run it – politicians and bureaucrats – interests that don't necessarily represent the majority of people. Appealing to people's self-interest is the strongest motive of all when it comes to maintaining your supporter base. In a democracy, it is the power of the party that vote in their leadership, who, in turn, are voted in by the people. In other words, politicians represent the interests of whoever keeps them in power. What politicians want, above all else, is to stay in office, and prosperity is essential to survival. A party of order and stability and a party of progress and reform are both necessary elements of a healthy political life, and economic stability is the key to political stability. As history has repeatedly demonstrated, widespread inflation and unemployment can quickly lead to xenophobia, intolerance, and fascism, as demonstrated in fascist Italy and Nazi Germany before World War II. It is economic growth that drives justice, freedom, and even happiness. A healthy economy is one that gives people a choice and a decent standard of living. A productive economy depends on its workforce being healthy and educated, and societies that nurture the pluralism of ideas, gender relations, and racial and ethnic engagement tend to be more innovative. Likewise, cultural diversity – which is open to different cultures, religions, and sexual orientations – plays a key role in economic growth and prosperity. Hence, your political ideology should embrace diversity as a necessary instrument of stability.

Good people skills, as we shall see, are fundamental to a successful political career because power is a collective responsibility. Political power requires the ability to build and maintain good relationships with a wide range of people who are fundamental to the political process. To maintain power, politicians give out privileges to certain groups in return for their political support. Don't think for one moment that you can rely on your general popularity with the people at large to give you a foothold in politics. A hugely popular sports star, musician, or actor does not necessarily translate to votes at the ballot box. While a well-known actor may have a head start over their political rivals in terms of recognition, they still need the support and endorsement of a major political party before they have any real chance of success at the ballot box. Rarely do high-profile celebrities who switch to politics ever win elections. However, what Hollywood actor turned Republican governor of California Arnold Schwarzenegger clearly demonstrated was the importance of belonging to an established major political party. The U.S. billionaire and 1990s presidential hopeful Ross Perot showed that no amount of money can buy you the votes you need for the top job if you don't align yourself with either of the major political parties. Donald Trump understood this very well when he decided to align himself with the Republican party for his successful tilt at the White House in 2016. Without the backing of an established major political party, money, talent, fame, and ability count for very little.

Outside the party, there are elder statesmen who can help you along your path to power. These are individuals who have experienced power themselves, so it is prudent to approach them as they may provide the springboard you need in your own quest for power. Having a respected senior or retired politician as a mentor is a critical activity that makes it possible to garner their sage advice. In the acclaimed BBC TV series *Yes Minister*, the ever-scheming Sir Humphrey Appleby always sought advice from his retired predecessor, Sir Arnold, especially when things got a little tricky for him. Advice from a trusted old hand in a relaxed setting such as an old-world gentleman's club is far removed from the frenetic scenes of cabinet room meetings, where self-interest and ambition may cloud a lively political debate. The elder statesman, like Sir Arnold, can play a pivotal role in your ascent to power. Surprisingly, many politicians often overlook the wise elder statesman when seeking advice and invariably repeat the same mistakes that were made in the past. Common sense will decree that if you ignore the lessons of history, then you are likely to fall into the same traps your predecessors endured. Elder statesmen are a wonderful repository of history because they have lived it from first-hand experience. Their intimate knowledge and circumspective view of history can provide essential clues that may expose hidden opportunities or warn against impending disaster.

Likewise, it may also be helpful to have people you can trust who are not part of the political process so that a person from outside the political arena can provide a caring and supportive role, especially during difficult and testing times. It may be your spouse, a retired work colleague, or an old professor, who can be surreptitiously approached as a sounding board that will help clarify your thinking on various issues, which is a technique U.S. president Abraham Lincoln often used to clear his thoughts before making important decisions. Trusted friends may provide a way through a stumbling block in times where your official advisers are divided or at a stalemate on certain issues. Mentors and friends are very much the unsung heroes of political leaders, and their support is crucial at times when the going gets tough and leaders need someone they can trust to lean on.

When Sen John F. Kennedy won the 1960 U.S. presidential elections, one of his first acts was to appoint his younger brother, Robert Kennedy, as attorney general, which their ambitious and politically savvy father, Joseph Kennedy, insisted on as a means of protection for the young president. Robert Kennedy fulfilled his role as the eyes and ears of the U.S. president and pulled no punches when it came to shielding his elder brother from hostile forces from within the Kennedy administration. Unfortunately, Robert's devotion failed to protect his brother from the assassin's bullets, which goes to show how unpredictable life can be. Sadly, we don't always have attentive brothers like Robert Kennedy to shield us from harm. We, therefore, must rely on trusted party colleagues to look out for dissent amongst the ranks. They act as your eyes and ears and should be able to sense if there is something not quite right. It may be something as innocuous as a subtle change in behaviour of certain members of your cabinet or executive council that is concealed from you but obvious to your supporters. People behave differently in front of their boss and rarely exhibit any behaviour that would concede their position. However, as many people know, subordinates can get up to great mischief behind the boss's back. So how does the boss keep these conniving people in check?

Close and trusted colleagues with a flair for exposing traitors amongst the ranks can be an essential asset for leaders who are too busy trying to run the country. However, leaders need to be careful and aware that those purporting to have your interests at heart do not have their own hidden agenda, which eliminates potential competitors to give themselves a free run for the top job. Joseph Stalin did precisely that when he out-manoeuvred the anointed successor Leon Trotsky following Lenin's brief reign over the newly declared Soviet state to take the top job after Lenin's death. Leon Trotsky (1879–1940), was a Russian Marxist revolutionary who joined the Bolsheviks immediately prior to the 1917 October Revolution. During the early days of the Soviet Union, he was a major figure in the Bolshevik victory and became a founding member of the Soviet politburo. Trotsky was second only to Vladimir Lenin. Although he had been groomed by Lenin to succeed him as leader, the wily Joseph Stalin successively removed Trotsky from power and had him deported from the Soviet Union and eventually assassinated. Intense rivalries can often harm the party, as ever sly and scheming Billy MacMahon showed when he took over the Australian prime ministership from a more capable John Gorton and ended up losing the 1972 election to Labour's Gough Whitlam after twenty-three years of conservative rule.

Political power requires the support of powerful colleagues, and this support must never be threatened by silly actions or deeds that may destabilise the bonds that hold your leadership together. A loss of support from key members of your party may threaten your power base and ultimately your leadership. Without the support and encouragement of your party colleagues, you become a lame duck leader. The game of politics is a game of cultivating and nurturing close relationships with powerful backers so that those responsible for keeping you in power are given no reason to depose you. Trusted party colleagues are your main line of defence and must be nourished with your attention and approval. Once success happens your way, the people you need to fear most are those colleagues, friends, and acquaintances you left behind. The dizzying heights of leadership can sometimes inadvertently break important alliances as leaders feel they have no further need for the colleagues that helped them to power. This is akin to cutting off your oxygen supply, and sooner or later, you will come gasping for air and discover that the colleagues you abandoned have abandoned you. Governing depends on understanding the important role of the people around you and how they represent the pillars of your support. Without them, you will fall. Your political power depends on cultivating the right alliances, and keeping them happy is vital to your success in the rough-and-tumble world of politics. Now that we have covered the importance of friendly alliances, let's turn our attention to potential enemies and how to manage them.

In October 1962, the USSR was covertly shipping nuclear missiles to Cuba, an island only ninety miles from the shores of the United States. U.S. spy planes flying over Cuba clearly showed intense construction activity on the ground in what appeared to be missile launch sites. The Americans were incensed by the prospect of hostile nuclear weapons at their doorstep and sent a clear ultimatum to the USSR to stop their activities or face the consequences. The Cuban Missile Crisis came very close to triggering a nuclear war between the superpowers, the United States and the USSR. Faced with the prospect of a nuclear Armageddon, the Soviet leader, Nikita Khrushchev, withdrew the nuclear missiles from Cuba. In response, the U.S. president, John F. Kennedy, made sure that the Soviets were given no reason to depose their leader because of his very public backdown. Instead, Kennedy ensured that it was Khrushchev who was given credit with the bold decision to avoid a nuclear war. As far as Kennedy was concerned, it was better to deal with the enemy he knew (i.e. Khrushchev) than with someone unknown, so it made sense to help Khrushchev save face and retain his leadership. It also helped that Kennedy and Khrushchev had met the previous year (1961) in Vienna, so the personal contact was a bonus that helped save the world from nuclear Armageddon. Former enemies expect nothing, so a man suddenly spared the firing squad is a grateful man indeed and would do anything for the man who pardoned him. Therefore, an important way to weaken your enemy is to do something totally unexpected, like calling an armistice even though you are on the cusp of victory. Sparing your enemies the indignity of total defeat may well change their attitude towards you.

It helps to appear candid as well as charming to your foes so that you make them believe that you can do business with them. You simply need to recognise their position and begin by finding common grounds for agreement. Find something that you both enjoy, such as golf or classical music, which helps moderate the tension between you. In a relaxed setting, you can disarm your opponent and subtly explore their inner workings, find out about their likes, dislikes, and other idiosyncrasies. If you get to know your opponent well, then you have a better chance of predicting how they will react to various situations so that you can counter or prevent belligerent responses. An understanding of people's hidden motives is the single greatest piece of knowledge you can have in acquiring power through advantage. Keeping your enemies close, you can secretly whittle away at their power base so when the time comes to cut them loose, they will fall fast and hard without knowing what hit them. You need to know your enemies well because they can inflict considerable damage if ignored and left unchecked. Never let the presence of enemies upset or distress you, for you are far better off with a sharply defined enemy than not knowing who your real enemies are. Powerful rulers welcome conflict because enemies can be used to enhance their reputation and keep them vigilant. Influencing what your opponent thinks about you is critical. The more attention your enemy pays you, the stronger you are made to look.

Never pick a fight with someone you are not sure you can defeat. If you are in a position of weakness, it is best to surrender than fight fruitlessly for the sake of honour. By yielding, you control the situation because you lull them into believing they have defeated you, but in fact, you have survived to fight another day. Conceal your intentions by telling your opponent what they want to hear and support ideas that may be contrary to your plans. Your moves must be planned and developed in the least obvious way, which disguises your cunning. That way, your enemy has no clue what you are up to, so they cannot prepare a defence. Deception using a smokescreen is the best strategy to distract people's attention from your real purpose. If you lead your opponent down a familiar path, he won't realise when you lead him into a trap. Approach your opponents with an ordinary idea and never appear over-passionate as you may raise suspicions.

Be wary of friends and colleagues who may betray you, for they are easily aroused to envy. Your most effective enemies can be your closest friends who understand your weaknesses. It is best to keep friends for friendship and work with the skilled and competent – i.e. don't hire friends. Behind any vehement hatred is often an underlying envy of the hated person or people. Toxic praise almost always indicates envy. Those who are hypercritical of you or who slander you publicly probably envy you as well. Do not try to help or do favours for those who envy you. Win your revenge by ignoring their measly presence and leaving them to stew in a hell of their own creation.

Known enemies – say, in opposition political parties – are easily kept in check. You recognise troublemakers by their overbearing presence or by their complaining nature. Once you spot them, do not try to reform or appease them. It is the hidden enemies within your own party that can inflict considerable damage. The effects of envy are more serious amongst colleagues and peers. Occasionally, you may be unaware of who your real enemies are until they launch their first attack against you and catch you by surprise. It is no wonder that history's archetypal tyrant, Joseph Stalin, eliminated many of his close associates who got too comfortable around him. His fear was that someone would topple him from within because he knew all too well that the most powerful enemy is the one well hidden within your ranks, someone who knew his weak points and could exploit these at the first opportunity. Sometimes internal enemies are best kept within your sphere of influence as it is easier to monitor their activities. Banishing enemies to the outer fringes gives them the freedom and opportunity to launch unrelenting attacks against you. By keeping them close, enemies are restrained by your loyal supporters and will find it very difficult to attack your policies when they are, in fact, part of your policy team.

In a democracy, opposition parties don't win elections. It is the incumbents that lose because in a contested election, what you should fear is not your opponent's strategy but your own mistakes. Therefore, it is the governing party that loses elections and often because of stagnation or internal divisions and infighting. The status quo is a dangerous place for the survival of political parties because complacency and stagnation are the ingredients of failure. Party unity is critical, and divisive cracks must be quickly patched up before they develop into rifts that split the party and invite enemy fire. Enemies like to prey on damaging internal rifts by fuelling them with mendacious smear campaigns which catch the attention of the media and the voting public. One of the chief reasons why the federal Australian Labour Party was out of office for more than two decades in the 1950s and 1960s was the rift that had developed between the left- and right-wing factions that resulted in the emergence of the right-leaning splinter group called the Democratic Labour Party (DLP). It was only when Gough Whitlam became Labour leader that he managed to restore unity and the party's credibility to win a belated Labour victory in the 1972 Australian federal elections.

It is better to find clever ways to neutralise your opponent's attacks than to hit back directly with similar attacks. Responding to mudslinging with more mud does nothing to help the situation. You do not want to leave everyone with the impression that you are just as bad as your opponents as you need to be seen to be above 'gutter'-style politics. To be in control, you need to be directing the events, not reacting to them. You need to keep the initiative and get others to react to your moves. When you force the other person to act, you are the one in control. So do not waste your energy in pursuit as you should lure them with bait and wait, for it is always better to make your opponent come to you. Malicious attacks require carefully planned surgical counterstrikes that put you in a dignified light and leave your opponent mortally wounded. If, for example, an opponent attacks you about your poor handling of the economy, find out whether this opponent of yours was ever bankrupted or had ever had any history of financial mismanagement that would neutralise his attack. When Donald Trump claimed U.S. president Barack Obama was not born in America, President Obama effectively neutralised Trump's allegations by targeting his Achilles' heel, challenging Trump to make public his tax records if Obama produced the birth certificate that confirmed he was born in Hawaii. Trump promptly disappeared off the radar.

The greatest example of how to deal with recalcitrant enemies was demonstrated during Ronald Reagan's presidency. He was credited with ending the Cold War by staring down his enemy – the Soviet Union. Ronald Wilson Reagan (1911–2004) was a radio, film, and television actor before he became governor of California (1967–1975) and then the fortieth president of the United States (1981–1989). Reagan was a tough president who survived an assassination attempt early in his presidency, which undoubtedly stiffened his resolve to take a hard line against all sorts of issues, including the Soviet Union, which he publicly called the 'evil empire' in a speech to the National Association of Evangelicals on 8 March 1983. He was so tough, he ordered military action against Grenada and the bombing of Libya just to show the world he would not shirk from hard decisions. He strongly supported anti-communist movements worldwide and ordered a massive military build-up in an arms race with the USSR by reversing the policy of détente, which began in 1979 under the Carter administration following the Soviet invasion of Afghanistan. Reagan's uncompromising stance and increased military spending escalated the Cold War, which was also fuelled by his hard-line policies towards the Soviet Union. In March 1983, Reagan introduced the Strategic Defence

Initiative (SDI), a defence shield to protect the United States from attack by strategic nuclear ballistic missiles that could make nuclear war impossible. Opponents dubbed the SDI 'Star Wars' and argued that the technological objective was unattainable, which was little comfort to the Soviet leader, Yuri Andropov, who became concerned about the possible consequences that the SDI would have on the balance of power between the two adversaries. For those reasons, many believe that the SDI may have hastened the end of the Cold War since the Soviets had no answer to the SDI conundrum.

The first American president ever to address the British Parliament on 8 June 1982, Reagan pronounced that 'the forward march of freedom and democracy will leave Marxism-Leninism on the ash heap of history'. On 3 March 1983, Reagan envisaged that communism would collapse, stating, 'Communism is another sad, bizarre chapter in human history whose last pages even now are being written.' Together with the UK's PM, Margaret Thatcher, Reagan denounced the Soviet Union in ideological terms and predicted that the Soviet Union's insatiable drive for military power would be eaten away by systemic failures intrinsic to communism that could not be reformed. In later years, Thatcher declared that 'Ronald Reagan . . . won the Cold War for liberty, and he did it without a shot being fired'.

When Mikhail Gorbachev came to power, there was a paradigm shift in the style of Soviet leadership which Reagan immediately recognised. Consequently, Reagan altered his hard-line stance and shifted to diplomacy to encourage the new Soviet leader to pursue significant arms agreements. Reagan wasted no time in initiating discussions on nuclear disarmament with General Secretary Gorbachev and held four summit conferences between 1985 and 1988. The summits culminated in the Intermediate-Range Nuclear Forces (INF) Treaty and the substantial reduction of the nuclear arsenals of both the United States and the USSR. By encouraging the Soviets to allow free speech and democracy, Reagan correctly predicted that this would lead to reform and the end of communism. When Reagan visited Moscow for the fourth summit in 1988, Reagan was optimistic about the new direction that he and Gorbachev had charted, which culminated in the fall of the Berlin Wall in November 1989 and the collapse of the Soviet Union two years later.

By the end of Reagan's presidency, over four decades of Cold War confrontation between the two superpowers had decreased dramatically, with many believing that Reagan's defence policies, hard-line stance against the Soviet Union and communism, and summits with Gorbachev played a significant part in ending the Cold War. While Reagan's foreign policies appeared aggressive, imperialistic, and 'warmongering', some argued that they were necessary to protect U.S. security interests. Gorbachev never acknowledged a win or loss in the Cold War but rather a peaceful end which perhaps signalled that communism's internal weakness had become so apparent that the Soviet Union would have collapsed in the end regardless of who was in power. Nevertheless, Reagan enters history as a leading player in the Cold War who played a major role in the collapse of communism. True to his on-screen cowboy image of a previous era, Reagan's tough persona reflected a resolve that enemies only respect tough opponents, and the Soviets knew they were no match for Reagan's determination to stare them down.

The true test of a political leader is found in the way they handle their enemies at the negotiating table. Insulting people is not a good way to foster useful dialogue and cooperation. With recalcitrant and stubborn people, work with what they give you instead of resisting and trying to change them. You look at the results of their actions, not what they say about their motivations. In any negotiation, be clear about where you stand from the beginning to help avoid the long-term erosion of trust when you backtrack on the expectation you created early on. You must know what you want from any deal, but to get there, you also need to be aware of what's at stake for the other person. The world would be a better place if we appreciated what we all have in common as opposed to focusing on the differences that only serve to divide us. Diplomacy is all about trying to reconcile rather than exaggerate differences. In any negotiation, agreeing with someone else's argument is disarming.

Negotiations should start by emphasising common ground. Talks break down when neither side gives way, so when dealing with a tough opponent, be prepared to make small concessions so that negotiations do not stall. A pragmatist avoids fights he cannot win and knows when to make compromises. We don't have to convince others that we're right. We just need to open their minds to the possibility that they may be wrong. If we approach disagreement as a contest, there will be winners and losers, but if we see it more as a dance, we can begin to choreograph a way forward. Furthermore, it is best to give your opponents options that come out in your favour, whichever one they choose. It is essential to keep your opponent firmly at the negotiating table and avoid remarks that may trigger a walkout. It pays to keep up dialogue with your enemies so that minor misunderstandings do not escalate into an all-out war. There is no benefit in public slanging because neither party looks good when relations become toxic. Avoid public confrontations and be the first to extend an olive branch of peace, which quickly makes your opponent look like the aggressor.

A good politician knows how to get things done by tactical retreats and compromise and by being more pragmatic and less idealistic. In recent years, Chinese diplomats under Xi Jinping's leadership have adopted an aggressive style of diplomacy dubbed 'wolf warrior diplomacy', which is blunt diplomacy that is both confrontational and combative. China defends wolf warrior diplomacy as a necessary response to any perceived criticism or slight of China arising from either foreign or domestic sources. Unfortunately, China's aggressive stance to all criticism, whether real or imagined, has tarnished its reputation and provoked a worldwide backlash that has left many countries feeling targeted and intimidated. This, in turn, has reduced China's standing in the world as a bullyboy who cannot be trusted, so countries are weary of doing business deals with China. History has shown that tyrannical governments spend huge resources in maintaining order and treat their people as a means towards an end. It is speculated that China's increased defence spending is more about control of its own population than to defend against external threats. Eventually, this belligerent behaviour will have regressive repercussions on China, which will leave it isolated and may have a devastating impact on its economy. China cannot afford to return to its isolationist policies, and so it must reign in its uncompromising attitude and start acting like a responsible superpower that is open for business. In short, Chinese diplomats should start acting like diplomats if they are going to succeed in developing a foreign policy with tangible benefits for the nation.

In any deal, there must be a win-win situation; otherwise, there is little point in discussions if the deal strongly favours one side. Your opponent's resolve to stand firm may be weakened if you concede first – on the clear understanding that any further concessions are dependent on your opponent's willingness to also concede until a comfortable level of agreement can be reached where both sides can walk away satisfied in the belief that they have made progress. If you approach your opponent with the attitude that you want to annihilate them, the feeling will be mutual, and mutually assured destruction can be the only outcome. Don't expect your enemies to easily capitulate with an unbridled display of brute force as there will be many casualties on both sides. By approaching your enemy with the intention of eliminating differences and finding some common ground, the encounter will be more fruitful and perhaps may even result in one less enemy. Keep in mind that enemies have much in common and much at stake, so the approach must be to keep your enemies close so that minor mishaps don't escalate into major calamities. All enemies are potential allies if you entice them with an offer they cannot refuse.

CHAPTER 5

Don't Upset or Burn Your Bridges

When a reporter asked U.S. president Ronald Reagan, during his first visit to the USSR, whether he still thought the Soviets were an 'evil empire', Reagan cleverly responded, 'No. That was another time, another era.' In those few clever words, Reagan acknowledged that positions taken in the past do not necessarily apply to the present, which ingeniously avoided the embarrassment of past declarations.

Friendships are important, but building bridges with influential people, companies, or organisations is essential. Bridge building is a fundamental priority of any ambitious politician who appreciates that the source of power can be unforgiving if you don't behave appropriately. Temper tantrums are poorly tolerated in politics. It is better to hold onto your anger for a day as time softens the emotion and can prevent you from saying or doing something stupid or destructive that you may inevitably regret. An angry person is more prone to feel suspicion, deep insecurities, and resentment. When your opponent is losing control, your tranquillity is a sign of strength, for it takes the wind out of their emotional sails. You also realise how easily you can undermine and take advantage of a person with so little self-control, for nothing is as infuriating as a man who keeps his cool while others are losing theirs. Childish temper tantrums by leaders are made worse in the presence of deputies who maintain their dignity and composure. People may be temporarily cowed by their boss's tantrums, but they ultimately lose respect.

To understand the true repercussions of losing your cool, you need to look no further than the fateful story of the hapless former Australian Labour leader Mark Latham. When Mark Latham (1961–) came to prominence at the age of forty-two, he became the youngest leader of the federal parliamentary Labour Party after Chris Watson in 1901. By the time he spat the dummy, Latham had been federal Labour leader for only thirteen months, the shortest tenure since Billy Hughes in 1916. In retrospect, Latham became leader perhaps too early in his career as he lacked the skills and experience needed to deal with complex relationships within his own party. His lack of respect for the media and the poor advice he did listen to hastened his downfall. The day before the October 2004 Australian federal election, Latham and John Howard, the incumbent PM, were filmed shaking hands as they crossed paths outside a radio studio in Sydney. In the encounter, Latham appeared to draw Howard towards him, appearing aggressive, bullying, and intimidating as he looked down menacingly over his shorter opponent. The incident received broad media attention which helped cast doubt on Mark Latham's personal style and subsequently resulted in a crisis in confidence in his leadership within the Labour caucus. After Labour lost the Australian federal election in October 2004, Mark Latham went into hiding, apparently to lick his wounds.

When the devastating tsunami struck the Indian Archipelago in Christmas 2004, there was not a word from Latham, who was still Labour leader. Latham was widely criticised for not issuing a statement as leader personally, particularly when John Howard expressed national sympathy over the disaster. Latham rejected the criticism, saying that 'none of my verbiage could make any practical difference – bring back the dead, reverse the waves, organise the relief effort'. When he did finally emerge on 18 January 2005, deteriorating relations with his party and ill health saw him resign as leader, and remarkably, he wasted no time in going on the attack against his own colleagues and party. He released a book, *The Latham Diaries*, in September 2005, which was scathing of many of his former colleagues and members of the media as well as the general state of political life in Australia. In the book, Latham was scornful of Australia's political system: 'It takes committed people . . . and turns them into one-dimensional robots . . . The only good news is that the public . . . can see through the spin doctors, the publicity stunts, the polling, and the tricks . . . [The electorate have] a clear feeling that the system is far from genuine.'

In a public lecture at Melbourne University on 27 September 2005, shortly after the release of *The Latham Diaries*, he argued that organised politics was ineffective at achieving real social change. He went on to say that political life is detrimental to health, happiness, and family life and blamed a conceited media and internal political party wrangling as the source of discontent. If there was any doubt that Latham would ever return to politics, his book made sure that there was not a hope in hell. When he departed the political arena, his firebrand approach to politics not only burned all bridges but made sure they were dynamited as well. The case of Mark Latham's precipitous descent from politics serves as an extraordinary reminder that injudiciousness can effectively destroy any hope of resurrecting one's career – and he didn't just destroy it. He made sure he annihilated it so that history would never know whether Mark Latham would have ever developed into a great leader or even PM had he chosen to follow a path very different from the one he took.

Another way to burn your bridges is to take a firm stance on issues. Political credibility relies on balancing ideology with pragmatism. Stupidity and ideology go very much hand in hand. Stupidity results from the claim to absolute knowledge or a single way to explain the world. Ideologies are simple ideas, disguised as science or philosophy, that purport to explain the complexity. All ideologies are prone to extremes, and ideologues are people who pretend they know how to make the world a better place. Ideologues are always dangerous when they come to power because the simple-minded 'I know it all' approach is no match for the complexity of existence. A good politician knows how to get things done by being more pragmatic and less idealistic. You don't burn your bridges simply because you think it makes you look tough. There is rarely a situation where you can confidently predict the future and take an unyielding stand today when the crucial facts that may make a mockery of your position are yet to emerge. In many instances, it may be safer to cast doubt on an issue than to firmly oppose it as it gives you the opportunity to revise your stance later. As opposition leader, it is better to go on public record as having said you have reservations about a new government tax, for example, rather than saying you would never support it and then, in government, introducing the new tax anyway. This is the ultimate in hypocrisy, and the media will never let you forget your original stance on the issue, which ultimately erodes your credibility. While politically, it may be a sign of strength and courage to take a stand, politicians need to leave themselves room to move to allow for changing circumstances. That way, you look more like a thoughtful leader than an assertive fool.

Policies are another important declaration that must be delivered in the light of current circumstances, with an escape clause in bold capitals suggesting that policies may need to be revised depending on unforeseeable events. Rules, regulations, and policies, when not thought through the lens of common sense, may actually result in unintended consequences. For instance, if a regulation takes away more than it achieves, get rid of it. Just before a general election, it is natural for opposition parties to promise the world to the electorate, regardless of cost. The desire to get something for nothing – or greed – is what blinds voters to the political swindler's tricks. The thought of a free lunch is the perfect bait for political votes, and yet, once in government, the promises made before the election are quietly dropped or radically pared back when the treasury balance sheet is finally laid bare. Surprises come in many forms, but clever politicians need to account for unforeseeable events by carefully choosing their words when announcing new initiatives or policies.

When it comes to unpopular decisions, seasoned politicians understand the need to clearly explain the merits behind their decision. Good politicians stay positive and stick to their message that tough decisions need to be made for the benefit of the nation. If, in the end, the message fails to get through, some political leaders make the fatal mistake of doggedly clinging onto their policies, fearing that any backdown may be a sign of weakness. Sometimes it is best to quit than to persevere with something that will not yield the results you may be looking for. British PM Margaret Thatcher was so hellbent on introducing the highly unpopular poll tax in 1990, she paid the ultimate price by losing her job. Policies that fail to garner popular support need to be seriously reviewed or quietly dropped from the public agenda, and one must move on. Even good public policy does not buy much loyalty because politicians essentially do what is most likely to keep them in power.

Climate change is another incredibly divisive issue that spawned the need for a carbon tax to help reduce man-made pollution that contributes to climate change. There are three positions adopted by those opposed to the carbon tax. By adopting the position of climate change denial, it makes you appear closed-minded and incapable of adjusting your thinking, even when the science supporting climate change is overwhelming. Rejecting the carbon tax in the belief that it makes no difference to climate change runs the risk of damaging your credibility if, when in government, you change your mind and decide to introduce it anyway because government revenue needs a boost. The climate change sceptic stance is the most appropriate for an opposition party to adopt because it provides a temporary position which can be conveniently exploited. That way, when you finally make it to government and you find that the treasury coffers need a boost, you can announce your change of heart without damaging your credibility by highlighting that the evidence for climate change is now overwhelming and you can now embrace the idea of a carbon tax. The former two options do not give you this opportunity to change your mind, whereas scepticism can easily turn to true believer if the facts are right, and the facts can be right at any time it suits the political party's agenda.

If you are to be trusted with the reins of government, then it is better to project an image of 'open-mindedness' in opposition by casting doubt than rejecting outright issues and the policies your party opposes. Without the benefit of a crystal ball, it is impossible to predict when you may need to adopt the very same policies in government that you vehemently rejected whilst in opposition. So don't burn your bridges because you never know when you may need to make an abrupt retreat, especially if you make a comment or take a stance that you may later regret. Hypocrites are easily exposed, and the public rarely forget politicians who say 'never, ever'. The media will make sure your stance on all matters and issues are recorded for posterity and given an airing every time they want to remind you of your 'never, ever' comment. So the safest position to take is to avoid the 'never, ever' and be a little circumspect when it comes to taking a stance on any issue that may come back to bite you. Burning your bridges leaves you no means of escape, and often your only step forward may be your final step into the political abyss. Speaking of political suicide, never upset those around you because you never know who may pull the trigger that leads to your ultimate downfall, as we shall now explore.

Influential people who are revered by many can cause the greatest damage if you upset them in any way. Treat these people with respect and be very careful, not only about what you say in their presence but also about what you say behind their back as there may be sly opportunists who are all too willing to betray your confidence. Some people get pleasure out of making others feel inferior, which is dangerous and counterproductive to relationships, especially with superiors. It is a mistake to think that you are charming people, like the king, with your natural talents when, in fact, they are coming to hate you. It is better to temporarily dull your brilliance than suffer the slings and arrows of envy. The naturally talented and perfect must work the most to hide their brilliance by displaying a defect or two to prevent envy from taking root and alienating their superiors, colleagues, and friends. It is unwise to insult or offend the intelligence or taste of people in power, even if they are below your own natural talents. To deflect envy, the powerful must display a harmless vice or weakness that rulers may connect with. Arrogant defiance can lose your head, especially as a subordinate who fails to toe the line. England's King Henry VIII had little tolerance when it came to insolent subordinates, like the hapless Sir Thomas More, Henry's former lord chancellor, who refused to take the oath to the king and was subsequently convicted of high treason and beheaded at Tower Hill, just outside the Tower of London. Fortunately, in the modern world, democratically elected leaders do not have the right to behead their subordinates when things don't quite go as planned. Public reprimand humiliates people and can easily turn supporters into foes. So it is best to admonish in private on a one-to-one level if someone needs to be set straight with constructive criticism and not threatening tirades. Leaders who want to maintain a strong supporter base need to keep their temper in check and ensure that those around them are treated with respect.

All people want to be taken seriously, which is the desire that goes to the very heart of who we are. So as a political leader, you must be cognisant of this frail human trait that can easily be exploited to your advantage. We have the embedded desire to be liked, respected, and paid attention to. We yearn for our individual place in this world where our unique role is recognised, valued, and accepted. By expressing modest admiration for other people's achievements, you paradoxically call attention to your own. If you constantly criticise others, some of that criticism will rub off on you. We are at our worst when we criticise others for the very frailties and shortcomings that we ourselves possess. Sometimes it takes one to know one. People hiding their insecurities will assert themselves a little too stridently. The way people defend against their own insecurity is to foster it in the people around them. When people overtly display some trait, such as confidence, they may often be concealing an opposite or contrary reality. Political leaders must be acutely aware of this amongst their staff so they know how to sensitively handle such people when they step out of line. Therefore, what often appears out of character may be more of their true character.

There are two ways you can influence human behaviour; you can manipulate it, or you can inspire it. It is always better to praise people for their effort, not their talent. The best strategy is to praise and flatter those qualities that people are most insecure about. A few flattering words aimed at their insecurities will melt their resistance, but never be too lavish in your praise as this will give away your insincerity. U.S. president Lyndon B. Johnson (1963–1969) was a master at flattery, particularly in the early stages of his political career. He would often come to meet with significant people with pen and paper in hand, ready to take down notes as he cunningly pretended to seek their advice. The road to influence and power is to let others be the star of the show, and when their defences are lowered, you can infect their minds with whatever ideas you want to insinuate. Johnson understood that by making them feel you appreciate their wisdom and experience, they will feel more relaxed in your presence and be more open to subtle manipulation and suggestions by planting ideas and influencing their behaviour. Asking people for advice implies that you respect their wisdom and experience, which Johnson knew would help forge important alliances with powerbrokers who would eventually catapult him to the highest office in the land.

As a leader, you rely on your deputies, your party, and your constituents for support. Deputies and all those closest to you in power have an intimate working knowledge of the powerbase that supports your leadership. So be careful about whom you insult because a man who is of little importance and means today can be a person of power tomorrow, and people never forget an insult. By publicly humiliating or upsetting those closest to you, you expose yourself to carefully targeted attacks that may hit at your Achilles' heel. Your closest colleagues know what keeps you in power, and they know how to inflict the maximum damage. They fully recognise the pillars that support your leadership and can effectively topple those pillars if you upset them in any way. J. Edgar Hoover, the notorious head of the Federal Bureau of Investigation (FBI), kept dossiers on all U.S. presidents and people in power for the express purpose of exposing embarrassing details if he felt that his job at the FBI was threatened. During the Kennedy administration in the early 1960s, Hoover clashed with Robert Kennedy, the attorney general and brother of the U.S. president. The Kennedys, however, were powerless to remove Hoover as they knew that Hoover had information that would destroy their respective careers. With unfettered access to enormous volumes of sensitive material, J. Edgar Hoover wielded considerable power, and few people were willing to cross him. It was no surprise that his death in 1972 was the only way to remove him from office. It is because he used the FBI to collect evidence using illegal methods, harass political dissenters and activists, and amass secret files on political leaders that FBI directors are now limited to ten-year terms.

In 1990, the British PM, Margaret Thatcher, was riding high on power, and after eleven years at the helm, she assumed she was invincible. So when she decided to ignore the advice of her deputies, it was the beginning of the end of her leadership. Thatcher's dictatorial leadership style, with her steadfast refusal to back down from the deeply unpopular 'poll tax' and views on the European Union, had undermined her reverence. By November 1990, she was unceremoniously pushed from office, not by the people but by her own party, who feared that her poor popularity in opinion polls was hurting the party. There is a fine line between heroic persistence and foolish stubbornness.

Baroness Margaret Hilda Thatcher (1925–2013) was the first woman to head a major UK political party when elected leader of the Conservatives in 1975, and in 1979, she became the UK's first female PM (1979–1990). Critics contend that Thatcher did 'little to advance the political cause of women' within her party. Her election followed a winter of discontent in Britain where rolling strikes had paralysed the nation. As PM, Thatcher was determined to reverse what she perceived as a precipitous national decline by revitalising Britain's economy and took a hard line against the trade unions. She supported deregulation, particularly of the financial sector, introduced flexible labour markets, and pursued the sale or closure of state-owned companies. Thatcher removed subsidies from 'outdated industries, whose markets were in terminal decline', which had created 'the culture of dependency', which had done such damage to Britain. She oversaw an increase in economic prosperity as total personal wealth rose by 80 per cent, with share ownership increased to a quarter of the adult population and two in every three families becoming proud owner-occupiers of their own homes.

Two of her most notable achievements are victory in the Falklands conflict and her strong alliance with the United States, in particular the special relationship she forged with the U.S. president Ronald Reagan. Thatcher survived two further elections but finally met her demise when her combative personality and willingness to override colleagues' opinions caused discontent within the Conservative Party. During her premiership,

Thatcher had the second lowest average approval rating, at 40 per cent, of any post-war PM. The tipping point came when she stood firmly by her Community Charge, which was widely unpopular amongst the electorate, and her views on the European community were not shared by others in her cabinet. On 1 November 1990, Geoffrey Howe, her longest serving cabinet minister, resigned as deputy PM over her stubborn refusal to agree to a timetable for Britain to join the European single currency. His resignation was fatal to Thatcher's premiership. She resigned as PM and party leader in November 1990 and was replaced as PM and party leader by her chancellor, John Major, who led the Conservatives to their fourth successive victory in April 1992. 'Thatcherism' has become a byword for nationalism, interest in the individual, and an uncompromising approach to achieving political goals, which has been adopted by subsequent governments, including Labour's Tony Blair.

Speaking of Labour leaders, Australia's Kevin Rudd deserves a mention as his autocratic style cut short his prime ministership because he managed to upset too many of his closest colleagues. Kevin Michael Rudd (1957–) was the twenty-sixth PM of Australia (2007–2010) and is, unhappily, the first Australian PM to be dumped from office by his own party during his first term in favour of his deputy, Julia Gillard. Despite the setback, Rudd can be proud to boast that in less than ten years, he went from backbencher to PM, quite a feat when you consider that the guy he toppled, John Howard, took more than two decades to reach the top job. Rudd grew up on a dairy farm in Queensland and joined the Australian Labour Party at the age of fifteen. He was elected to the federal House of Representatives in 1998 as the Australian Labour Party member for Griffith, Queensland, and was quickly promoted to the Labour frontbench in 2001 as shadow minister for foreign affairs. In no time at all, he was thrusted to lead the Labour Party in December 2006 and became PM within a year after Labour won a belated election victory at the federal elections in 2007 with a twenty-three-seat swing against the incumbent Liberal/National Party coalition government. Once in government, Rudd wasted little time in signing the Kyoto Protocol and delivering a long overdue apology to Indigenous Australians for the stolen generations. He dismantled WorkChoices, the previous government's industrial relations legislation, and withdrew Australia's remaining Iraq War combat personnel. Australia became one of the few Western countries to avoid the 2008 recession when the Rudd government provided economic stimulus packages in response to the global financial crisis. Rudd rode a wave of popularity in the opinion polls, and during their first two years in office, Rudd and his government set records for popularity in Newspoll polling. So what went wrong?

Unfortunately, Kevin Rudd was a hot-headed and temperamental leader who created enormous stress for those who worked for him. By 2010, Rudd's approval ratings plummeted as controversies stirred over the incompetent and wasteful management of the economic stimulus following the global financial crisis. To add to his woes, leaks from U.S. diplomatic cables described Rudd as a 'control freak' and 'a micro-manager' obsessed with managing the media cycle rather than engaging in collaborative decision making. Rudd's propensity to make 'snap announcements' without consulting the Australian government or foreign countries also came in for criticism from foreign diplomats who had dealt with him in foreign policy matters. It became clear that many in the Labour Party caucus felt ignored by Rudd's centralist leadership style. His insulting and rude treatment of subordinates and other ministers was initially tolerated because of his immense popularity with voters. However, when Rudd's poll numbers began to drop in late 2009 and early 2010, his own party felt that they had had enough of his autocratic style and quickly moved to clip his wings and remove him from the top job. A precipitous decline in the opinion polls and growing dissatisfaction of his leadership style within the Labour Party triggered a leadership challenge by his deputy, Julia Gillard. On 24 June 2010, realising he didn't have the numbers if he contested the leadership, Rudd stepped down as party leader and PM before the ballot was called. Kevin Rudd's rapid political ascent was matched by an even greater precipitous political decline because as leader, he failed to realise that his power came from his party and not the electorate. Rudd's story is emblematic of what happens when you upset those nearest you and treat them with contempt.

The voting public expect their leaders to behave appropriately and show a sense of pride in the people they work with. Being decent to people and treating everyone with fairness and respect creates an environment where people know you'll hear them out and so will not be afraid to approach you with problems that require your input. Judging people too harshly generates fear and anxiety, which discourages communication. As clearly demonstrated by Kevin Rudd's demise, Western politicians who treat people badly do not survive very long in the top job. Following the golden rule of treating people as you would like to be treated will ensure respect and harmony amongst your workforce. No one wants to work for tyrants or short-tempered individuals – unless, of course, your boss is a dictator of a country in terminal decline and you are one of the few privileged citizens with a job and a decent salary. Western political leaders who show only contempt for those they work with will quickly discover how precarious their powerbase is and will find few supporters in times when they need them most.

Politicians should also never forget their own constituents. These are the people who voted for them, and they need their support at every election. Therefore, it is essential that their interests are upheld because political leaders who make decisions that benefit the nation as a whole but harm their own constituents will either need to look for another electoral seat or another job at the next election. For example, if your electoral boundary includes a massive car plant that employs hundreds of locals, which sustains a large part of the local economy, then signing an executive order which reduces tariffs on imported cars will be akin to signing your own political death certificate. While most people will benefit from lower car prices when tariffs are reduced, politicians will not receive mountains of congratulatory letters from their grateful nation. Instead, political leaders should expect lots of hate mail from a small but vocal group of local car manufacturers and their employees adversely affected by the tariff reduction. If you rely on their support to stay in power, avoid antagonising small interest groups closely connected to your supporter base who may destabilise your position if you do anything to upset them.

So in summary, never take your exalted position for granted as appearing superior to your colleagues and treating them with disdain is not only stupid but also fatal. In the presence of your colleagues and when you are just starting out in your political career, you should always disguise your strengths, act naive, and make your boss appear more intelligent than you by seeming to ask for his expertise. Power requires a wide and solid support base, which envy and conflict can silently destroy. Envy creates silent enemies, especially when you appear better than others and openly flaunt your talents and success. It takes great talent and skill to conceal one's talent and skill because envy is a weed that should not be watered.

Chapter 6

Perception and Lies

How a piece of information is framed influences the way it is perceived. Presentation greatly matters; a potential outcome framed as a loss will have more impact than if it is presented as a gain. Pessimism just sounds much smarter and more plausible than optimism. Tell someone they will be great, and they shrug you off, but tell them that they are in danger, and you have their undivided attention. Furthermore, our response is affected by how the decision is presented. If it is presented as a loss, we prefer to gamble, but if it is presented as a gain, we choose the sure thing. Experienced politicians can readily manipulate the opinions and choices of the masses by framing their narratives in a way that nudges people towards their way of thinking.

To attract attention, you must do something different and odd, for crowds are attracted by the unusual and inexplicable. Society craves larger-than-life figures, people who are far from predictable and are in control by playing against their expectations. In modern politics, success depends on a leader's ability to impress, fascinate, and engage the public with an air of mystery. An air of mystery heightens your presence and creates anticipation. If you are too present and familiar, always available, and visible, you will seem too banal. As a leader, you want to be more mysterious, to establish a presence that fascinates people. You may achieve this by making yourself scarce and only appear when necessary so that it creates excitement and anticipation amongst your followers. Powerful people impress and intimidate by saying less, which makes them appear profound and mysterious. Your silence will make other people uncomfortable, and short responses will put them on the defensive. The more you say, the more likely you are to say something foolish or unintended. A person who cannot control his words is unworthy of respect because he cannot control himself.

The verbose are often perceived as helpless and unsophisticated because by talking more, they expose their weaknesses. All great leaders know that an aura of mystery draws attention to them and creates an intimidating presence. For them to make themselves less obvious, what they reveal causes excitement, and what they conceal heightens interest. Mao Tse-tung cleverly cultivated an enigmatic image by teasing and titillating with alluring and even inconsistent and contradictory comments which appealed to the population to try and make sense of it all. The artist Andy Warhol rarely talked about his work; he let others do the interpreting because the less an artist talks about his work, the more people talk about it, and the more they talk, the more valuable his work becomes. By saying less than necessary, you create the appearance of meaning and power. We are enthralled by mystery because it invites constant interpretation, excites our imagination, and induces us into believing that it conceals something marvellous. An air of mystery can make the mediocre appear intelligent and profound, and for an aspiring politician, it immediately makes their persona more intriguing. North Korea's Kim Jong-un has taken a leaf out of Mao's rule book on how supreme leaders can make themselves appear to be more intelligent than what they really are.

In a democracy, a political leader must cultivate a public image that puts them in the best possible light. Politicians must avoid ever seeming petty, self-serving, or indecisive. A happy, smiling politician is always reassuring, which is tempered during serious or solemn occasions such as state funerals or natural disasters. Even a nervous smile during a visit to emergency headquarters may be interpreted as totally inappropriate as it shows a lack of compassion for those affected by the natural disaster. Politicians who are heckled by bystanders during a public walkabout is a regular part of democratic political life. Heckling is a good indicator of democracy at work as the heckler is simply exercising his right to speak his mind. Politicians must accept these awkward moments as an ordinary act of democracy and should keep walking without concern. Alternatively, if cornered with no escape route and the TV cameras are there to capture the very moment, then it's best to turn the tables on the heckler by putting them in the spotlight with questions of your own. Revealing questions like

'What do you think should be done?' will quickly expose those who have a genuine grievance and those who were planted there by the opposition.

People want their leaders to listen to them. It is their five minutes of fame and a golden opportunity to tell their leaders what they think. Politicians should step back and give the poor punter the limelight as it shows that the politician really listens to their people. Never start an argument with members of the public while in full view of the press. Just simply thank them for their comments and move on. If it is a genuine grievance, add that you will investigate it. Never offer detailed explanations, solutions, or reasons unless it conforms to the message you had intended to convey to the media and general public on the day. One incident which rattled the former Australian Labour PM Bob Hawke was when he was confronted by an elderly pensioner during a walkabout in Adelaide in the 1980s. Unfortunately, the tirades from the elderly bloke got to the PM, and in front of all the TV cameras, the PM called him a 'silly bugger' and walked off. It became primetime television viewing that night, and the insult delivered by the PM on the poor old pensioner with a grievance shattered the persona of Bob Hawke as a people's PM. The spin doctors acted quickly, and in no time, Bob was back on screen apologising unreservedly for the verbal insult, which the press had interpreted as an attack on the Australian people and an affront to free speech.

As a politician, you are often on the back foot when public appearances don't follow a script. Australia's longest serving PM, the late Robert Menzies, was a natural player when it came to dealing with hecklers. In the 1950s and 1960s, the press were less scrutinising, and public gatherings were riotous affairs, unlike the carefully scripted public appearances of contemporary politicians. At one town hall meeting in Williamstown, Victoria, in 1954, a spirited heckler shouted at Menzies, 'I wouldn't vote for you if you were the Archangel Gabriel!' In a jocular tone, Menzies coolly replied, 'If I were the Archangel Gabriel, I'm afraid you wouldn't be in my constituency,' which sent the crowds into fits of laughter. This quick-witted response in chaotic situations gave Menzies the aura of unperturbed confidence and supreme control, which reassured people that he was the right man for the job of leading the country.

Sir Robert Gordon Menzies (1894–1978) was the longest serving PM of Australia when, for a second time, he became PM at the 1949 election and dominated Australian politics, as no other person has, until his retirement in 1966. During Menzies's long reign, Australia became an increasingly affluent society. It has been said that the long post-war economic boom and his clever exploitation of anti-communist fears in the Cold War years were the main reasons for Menzies's success. Menzies was renowned as a brilliant speaker, both on the floor of parliament and on the hustings, which highlighted to the public at large his oratorical skills. His most famous speech, 'The Forgotten People', was first broadcast to the nation in May 1942 during the height of the Second World War. The speech defined the middle class as the backbone of Australia, which had been ignored by political parties because they lacked an organised voice, which Menzies cleverly used as the values that would form the basis of the Liberal Party of Australia. The best remembered part of the speech, delivered on 22 May 1942, went as follows:

> ' I do not believe that the real life of this nation is to be found either in great luxury hotels and the petty gossip of so-called fashionable suburbs or in the officialdom of the organised masses. It is to be found in the homes of people who are nameless and unadvertised and who, whatever their individual religious conviction or dogma, see in their children their greatest contribution to the immortality of their race. The home is the foundation of sanity and sobriety. It is the indispensable condition of continuity. Its health determines the health of society as a whole.

Menzies was PM for a total of eighteen years, by far the longest term of any Australian PM. He remains highly regarded in Australian history as a legend in Australian politics. Like Menzies, politicians need to be seen as confident leaders who are comfortable in their role of leading their nation. Perception is everything, and leaders need to show their people that they are the right person for the job. Everything about a leader – their appearance, their dress sense, their smile, and their oratory skills – must exude leadership qualities that resonate with people's expectations.

There is often a gap between what people say they like (stated preferences) and the actual preferences they express when forced to make a real choice (revealed preferences). You can ask people what they like, but you won't get nearly as honest an answer as when you observe what they are actually doing. Perception is therefore a product of deeds, not just words, where political power is earned through actions, not just speeches, that show leadership qualities such as courage, vision, strength, and integrity. Your success in politics will be determined by how you respond to punctuated moments of crises, not years spent on cruise control. The ability to maintain calm and resilience in the face of adversity is what separates a good leader from the rest. An effective leader must remain optimistic, especially during challenging times, and be able to encourage, reward, and praise his people so that loyalty remains strong.

Strength of leadership was shown during the Roosevelt administration in the 1930s and 1940s, where U.S. president Franklin Roosevelt cleverly hid his physical disability from the public so that it did not distract the people from confronting, head on, the terrible issues they had to face in the Great Depression and Second World War. Franklin Delano Roosevelt (1882–1945), often referred to as FDR, was the longest serving president of the United States. He was elected during the depths of the Great Depression in 1933 and served four terms as president until his death in office just before the end of the Second World War in 1945. Roosevelt was struck down by a debilitating illness which made him a paraplegic, yet in public newsreels, he was often shown in the standing position. In August 1921, Roosevelt contracted polio while vacationing with his family at Campobello Island in Canada. The illness resulted in permanent paralysis from the waist down and left him a paraplegic, which Roosevelt carefully concealed from the public. He was considered as the most famous polio survivor, and after he became president, he helped establish the March of Dimes, a national foundation for infantile paralysis. Roosevelt refused to accept that he was permanently paralysed and tried a wide range of therapies. To run for public office, FDR was able to convince many people that the paralysis was only temporary and that he was getting better. He took great care to shield his disability from the press by never being seen in public in a wheelchair. In front of crowds and the gathered media, he always appeared standing upright with the aid of iron braces fitted to his hips and legs and supported on either side by an aide or one of his sons. He took great pains in teaching himself to walk short distances by swivelling his torso while supporting himself with a cane. His car had specially designed hand controls which gave him greater mobility. It was obvious that FDR did not want his physical disability to be seen as a sign of weakness in the public eye and was determined to show his strength of leadership even if it meant wearing painful and uncomfortable iron braces.

FDR's leadership during a time of global economic crisis and world war and his accomplishments made him a towering figure in world events during the mid-twentieth century. Franklin Roosevelt's success as a politician was because no one could read his face. He bolstered the national spirit with his optimism and activism when he defeated the incumbent Republican Herbert Hoover in November 1932. Because of the two major crises that confronted Roosevelt's presidency, he expanded government social programmes which helped redefine the role of government and liberalism in the United States for coming generations. The 'Four Freedoms' speech firmly established the active leadership role of the United States in the global war and on the world stage. His close alliance with Winston Churchill and the Soviet dictator, Joseph Stalin, was pivotal in the Allied victory against Germany and Japan in World War II, but sadly, he died on the eve of final victory over Germany on 12 April 1945. With his dominance of the American political scene and diplomatic impact on the world stage which resonated long after his death, Roosevelt is rated one of the top three U.S. presidents in the history of the United States. Having guided his nation through the Great Depression and World War II and into prosperity, his biographer, Jean Edward Smith, cleverly remarked, 'He lifted himself from a wheelchair to lift the nation from its knees.'

A disabled president confined to a wheelchair would not have inspired confidence in a nation tormented by economic crises and world war. FDR lived during times where the strength of leadership could only be projected to the public by careful manipulation of his image, free of the distractions of a physical disability. Unfortunately, contemporary media is more scrupulous than it was during FDR's time. In their battle to sell more newspapers and improve their audience ratings, media outlets are more inclined to target and expose political scandals than good news stories. If FDR had lived in today's world, there would no doubt be countless news stories written about his disability, which would most likely have made it impossible for him to run for the highest office in the land. Public perception depends on how you engage the public through the media, which FDR successfully manipulated to his advantage. The power of exceptional oratory skills is the most effective way of convincing people that you are the right person for the top job. Public speaking and parliamentary debate are key proficiencies that all aspiring politicians must nurture and develop to perfection as both these abilities are largely what the media and public judge you on. History often cites famous political figures who are best remembered not only for their speeches but also for whether their words are reflected in their actual deeds. A positive public perception is all about projecting the right public image, and the ability to manipulate the truth is the foundation that supports it, as we shall now explore in further detail.

When people feel frightened or insecure, a politician's grip on power becomes more secure. Politics feeds off people's fears; that is why governments tend to benefit from a population's fears. Politicians love nothing more than an enemy as a focus of our fears – be it communism or terrorism, real or imagined – for it is well known that a person who can spin a fantasy out of an oppressive reality has access to untold power. As a forger of fantasies, let your victim come close enough to be tempted, but keep him far enough away so that he stays dreaming. Those who promise a great and total change from misery to ecstasy will have a great many followers. In other words, have a mad vision, and you're a kook. Get a crowd to believe in it, and you're a supreme leader.

The Romans judged their political system by asking not whether it made sense but whether it worked, regardless of the truth. All reality outside the natural sciences is socially constructed, so the aim of social sciences such as law and politics is not to discover the truth but to persuade people of the truth. Likewise, clever politicians don't use their intellect to obtain the correct answer; they use it to obtain what they want the answer to be. All kinds of public debate in which statistics and economic data are routinely invented or manipulated and contrary data ignored are inappropriately exploited by politicians and bureaucrats and lawyers for their vested interests to pursue self-serving agendas. For example, lawyers will look for 'expert opinions' that match their agenda so that evidence-based knowledge is totally ignored. Journalists, politicians, and lawyers have little concern for the truth in their effort to score points to impress their uninformed readership, electorate, or jury, respectively. Accordingly, there are no true or false arguments, only persuasive and unpersuasive ones. What matters more than the truth is persuasion and manipulation, so the priority of a politician is persuasion, not sincerity. It is, therefore, not surprising that the public perceive most politicians as fundamentally flawed characters, such as being dishonest or insincere, which shows in people's distrust of them, and everything they do is perceived as being manipulative.

Truth is something that politicians find very hard to grapple with because political candidates who are not willing to cheat or lie are typically beaten by those who are. Politicians are driven by vested interests, so disinformation and distraction become essential survival tactics. People tend to jump to conclusions based on limited evidence because knowing little makes it easier for cunning politicians to put together a compelling story. Missing bits of the puzzle doesn't seem to matter because we are inclined to believe that what we see and hear from authorities is all there is. Humans are incorrigibly inconsistent in making summary judgements of complex information which politicians can easily exploit. The most useful knowledge is one that changes behaviour, and the real test of knowledge is not whether it is true but whether it empowers us to control the thoughts and opinions of others.

Simple repetition can be the most powerful strategy used to boost a statement's truthfulness provided the message is simple and fits with people's existing opinions to sway the argument in the politician's favour. Being selective in the evidence they present, clever politicians package it in an easy-to-understand sound bite that is intended to muddy the truth. When caught in a lie, the more emotional and certain you appear, the less likely it will appear that you are lying. If you believe in the lie, you are less likely to give yourself away as a liar to others, and the way to do it is called conviction. A man with a conviction is difficult to change. Show him the facts, and he questions your sources. Appeal to logic, and he cannot see your point. When reality clashes with his deepest convictions, he fails to amend his worldview regardless of the evidence. With every attack, he becomes even more rigid in his beliefs than before. Does it sound familiar? The U.S. gun lobby use this tactic all the time. In this respect, a determined individual with a political agenda will always find this tactic useful in neutralising opposing views because their opponent simply gives up.

The greatest truths in life are usually the most unpleasant to hear. According to Nietzsche, a man's worth is determined by how much truth he can tolerate. The truth can often be cold, sober, and uncomfortable, whilst a lie can be a lot more palatable. People do not want the truth; they just want support and confirmation. Wise and clever politicians learn early on that they can display conventional behaviour and mouth conventional ideas without having to believe in them. With time and experience, politicians do not change what they believe; rather, they become better actors. Your outward conformity gives you the freedom to work unhindered, without having to change your thinking, ideas, and values. It is invaluable to be all things to all people, so when you go into society, put on a mask that is most appropriate for the group in which you find yourself. Stay with the herd, for there is safety in numbers. Keep your differences in your head and not on your sleeve so that the truth is surreptitiously sacrificed in the pursuit of your political goals.

It is much harder to hide a lie when everyone is honest. Therefore, cheating is harder to get away with if you are the only one cheating. The best place to hide a lie is in a place full of liars. So we are more likely to get away with a lie when everyone else is lying and cheating. The key is how to lie without being exposed. In politics, power is infinitely more important than the truth. For politicians, the truth is whatever is politically convenient at that moment. To win the war, politicians would never tell the truth if a lie would serve them just as well. For instance, effective politicians never promise gradual improvement through hard work; rather, they promise the moon, the great and sudden transformation, the pot of gold, which vulnerable people gladly soak up without a second thought. 'I would certainly vote for him because it sounds like a once-in-a-lifetime offer you would be crazy to refuse, right?' It is amazing how people easily forget that if it is too good to be true, then it is, which is an astonishing reality that most of us prefer to ignore.

A lie is simply deception, and the essence of deception is distraction. When it is nearly impossible to tell what is being said, almost anything can be said because exceptionally dishonest arguments can be smuggled in under the guise of complexity. The one thing that all purveyors of social justice have in common is that their work is incomprehensible. Take Karl Marx's *Communist Manifesto*, for example. His writing has an obstructive style usually employed when someone either has nothing to say or needs to conceal the fact that what they are saying is not true. Distracting the people you want to deceive gives you the opportunity to do something they won't notice. For example, a gift is the perfect object in which to hide a deceptive motive. The act of honesty, kindness, or generosity is often the most powerful distraction because it disarms other people's suspicions. The paranoid and weary are often the easiest to deceive. Win their trust in one area, and you effectively blind their view in another. Drawing attention to the familiar, bland, and inconspicuous blinds people to the deception being perpetrated behind their backs. To stop themselves from openly lying, experienced political pundits skirt around tricky situations by ignoring questions, answering imaginary questions, or simply changing the subject altogether. It is fascinating to watch seasoned reporters asking pointed questions and how politicians deliberately dodge the answer until the reporter gives up and moves on to the next question. Live interviews are better than pre-recorded interviews because politicians know the reporter has strictly limited time to pose the necessary questions. So by deliberately wasting the limited time skirting around the issues, experienced politicians avoid answering the tough questions. If, on the other hand, you are fishing for information, it is usually quite easy to get people to open up by asking them about themselves. To extract secrets out of people in polite conversation, you need to suppress yourself in conversation to make others talk endlessly about themselves. Ask indirect questions to get people to reveal their weaknesses and intentions. For stubborn people, give them a false confession, and they will give you a real one. If people are trying to cover something up, they tend to become extra vehement, righteous, and chatty. They defend themselves with an intense level of denial. An overt trait can sometimes hide an underlying secret. For example, an openly homophobic person may well be a suppressed homosexual and so on.

People lie to friends, to surveys, and to themselves to make themselves look better. There are many kinds of lies perpetrated by all of us in the course of our social exchanges with family, friends, neighbours, workmates, customers, or strangers. While lies are often seen as immoral and damaging, there are occasions where lies are required as a means to an end that, paradoxically, may be useful in deliberately avoiding dire consequences. There's more on that later, but first, let's take a look at the big barefaced lies those unsavoury political leaders weave as a means of gaining personal advantage.

Politicians who are in the spotlight are often on public record, and so the statements they make either to the media or in the parliament are recorded for posterity. This, of course, only applies to sovereign nations where there is a free media. As we shall see, the media can either collude with political leaders to hide unsavoury truths from the public, as in the case of the legendary infidelities of U.S. president John F. Kennedy, or be unforgiving and tenacious in its pursuit of the truth, as was the case of the Nixon Watergate scandal in the 1970s. Occasionally, a political leader with a dark secret comes along and manages to survive with their credibility intact, as Ronald Reagan managed to do with the Iran–Contra affair. U.S. president Ronald Reagan was a master at delivering speeches that appeared very natural and relaxed, even when he lied. In fact, Reagan has been labelled by historians as the great communicator. He was so good at delivering speeches that in 1986, he even managed to save his presidency from the Iran–Contra affair, where American hostages were illegally swapped for arms, by telling the American people that if he knew what he did was wrong, then he didn't mean to do it, and funnily enough, they forgave him. He no doubt put his previous movie acting skills to good use. Unfortunately for U.S. president Richard Nixon, he wasn't so lucky, and, as we shall see, his persona did little to help his cause when he tried to cover up the Watergate scandal and was forced to quit under the threat of impeachment.

Richard Milhous Nixon (1913–1994) was the thirty-seventh president of the United States (1969–1974), and he remains the only U.S. president in history to resign from office. After leaving office, Nixon spent the next twenty years of his life trying to rehabilitate his image. While Nixon is largely remembered for the Watergate scandal, as U.S. president, he achieved many things. First, he inherited the Vietnam War, which he finally brought to a conclusion after ten years of bitter conflict which saw fifty-five thousand young American troops killed by the time he successfully negotiated a ceasefire with North Vietnam in 1973, effectively ending American involvement in the war. Nixon's ground-breaking visit to the People's Republic of China in 1972 opened diplomatic relations between the United States and China, and he initiated détente and forged the Anti-Ballistic Missile Treaty with the Soviet Union. On the domestic front, he abolished the gold standard, introduced sweeping environmental reforms by creating the U.S. Environmental Protection Agency, launched the war on cancer and war on drugs, and pushed for the desegregation of schools in the deep South. He was re-elected by a landslide in 1972 but soon after was embroiled in the 'Watergate' scandal, which overshadowed his many reforms in his second term in office.

On 17 June 1972, five men were caught breaking into Democratic Party headquarters at the Watergate Hotel in Washington, D.C. The men were linked to the Nixon White House after two newspaper reporters from the *Washington Post* picked up the story from an FBI informant known as 'Deep Throat', who revealed a series of scandalous acts involving the Committee to Re-elect the President. Watergate became a news sensation when it was soon realised that the illegal and secret activities surrounding the break-in were undertaken by members of the Nixon administration. When it became evident that Nixon aides had attempted to sabotage the Democrats, Nixon downplayed the scandal as politics and denounced the story, but his rebuttal failed to stem the tide of resignations as senior aides faced prosecution over the affair. Matters turned for the worse when senior aide John Dean testified that Nixon had ordered a cover-up and another aide, Alexander Butterfield, revealed that Nixon had a secret taping system that recorded his conversations and phone calls in the Oval Office. The tapes were promptly subpoenaed, but the White House refused to release them, so a tentative deal was struck for the White House to provide written summaries of the tapes, which was rejected by Special Prosecutor Archibald Cox. Eventually, an audio tape surfaced of conversations held in the White House on 20 June 1972 which featured an unexplained eighteen-and-a-half-minute gap, which fuelled further suspicion and cast doubt on Nixon's claim that he was unaware of the cover-up. In the face of plummeting popular support, he vowed to stay in office, insisting he had no prior knowledge of the burglary, did not break any laws, and did not learn of the cover-up until early 1973. In a televised interview in November 1973, Nixon said, 'People have got to know whether or not their president is a crook. Well, I'm not a crook. I've earned everything I've got.'

The final nail in the coffin for Nixon came when one of the secret recordings, known as the 'smoking gun' tape, was released on 5 August 1974 and revealed that Nixon knew of the cover-up from its inception. In the tapes, Nixon had suggested to administration officials that they try to stop the FBI's investigation. His position became untenable, and in the face of likely impeachment for his role in the Watergate scandal, Nixon resigned on 9 August 1974, after addressing the nation on television the night before. In his final address to the nation, he never admitted to criminal wrongdoing, although he conceded errors of judgement. Following his resignation, Nixon returned to his home, La Casa Pacifica, in San Clemente, California, with little to do but suffer as a tormented soul as he felt he had so much more work left to do as president. Nixon subsequently released a statement:

> I was wrong in not acting more decisively and more
> forthrightly in dealing with Watergate, particularly when
> it reached the stage of judicial proceedings and grew from
> a political scandal into a national tragedy. No words can
> describe the depth of my regret and pain at the anguish
> my mistakes over Watergate have caused the nation and

the presidency, a nation I so deeply love and an institution
I so greatly respect.

He was later controversially pardoned by his successor, Gerald Ford, for any federal crimes he may have committed while in office, which ended any possibility of indictment and put an end to the desire amongst many in Congress and the media to see him punished. The pardon was based on a statement of remorse from a reluctant Nixon, who maintained that he did not commit any crimes. Nixon had a complex personality that was both awkward and secretive, and he was inclined to distance himself from people because of his uncomfortable shyness and paranoia. His drive, diligence, and tenacity masked a deep unease where he believed he was a misunderstood and underappreciated person who would be betrayed and unjustly harassed. In his account of the Nixon presidency, author Richard Reeves described Nixon as 'a strange man . . . [who] assumed the worst in people, and he brought out the worst in them.' The way we see the world effectively describes who we are. So if we are good, we see goodness in the world. If we are bad, all we see is badness in the world, which is how Nixon saw the world. Former president Harry Truman had a poor regard for Nixon, stating in 1961, 'Nixon is a shifty-eyed goddamn liar, and the people know it.' In 1968, he added, 'He's one of the few in the history of this country to run for high office talking out of both sides of his mouth at the same time and lying out of both sides.' Martha Mitchell, the outspoken wife of Nixon's attorney-general John Mitchell, said of Nixon in 1973, 'He bleeds people. He draws every drop of blood and then drops them from a cliff. He'll blame any person he can put his foot on.'

Nixon's presidency was doomed by his personality and the public perception of it, which was reflected in cartoon caricatures which exaggerated Nixon's shifty appearance and suspicious mannerisms. Many years later, John W. Dean, who served as Nixon's counsel from 1970 to 1973, remarked that Nixon was his own worse problem and that his finest act as U.S. president was to resign. People just couldn't trust him, and the Watergate affair only served to confirm the popular perception that Richard Nixon deserved the title of 'Tricky Dick'. Nixon's legacy demonstrates that without integrity, a leader will fall on his sword. In response to the possibility of a bribe being extorted by those convicted in the Watergate break-in, Nixon's response was clearly that of a leader without any moral convictions when he told his aide that the money could be found. This not only horrified the aide but also clearly showed that Nixon had no scruples when it came to dodgy deals that would shield his criminal activities from the public at large. Nixon not only destroyed himself but also took many others down with him during his blemished presidency.

While the intention of lying is to deceive others, not all lying is immoral. A savvy politician who needs to hide the truth can resort to be economical with the truth – that is, he may deliberately hold back relevant details and not reveal too much information by being very careful with the facts. This may be especially useful in times of a national crisis to help maintain law, order, and safety. When the Fukushima Nuclear Plant was hit by a massive tsunami following an earthquake in northern Japan in early 2011, the government deliberately played down the level of dangerous radiation leakage to prevent mass panic and evacuation of the surrounding township as aid to other earthquake-stricken places in Japan was already overstretched. The government decided that it was better to keep the residents in their own homes than to create more refugees for an already overstretched aid response.

Outside a crisis, political leaders are sometimes compelled to lie to their own people to achieve certain aims. The most celebrated lie is a fabrication which is projected as being true without knowing for certain whether it is actually true or not. During World War II, Hitler's right-hand man, Joseph Goebbels, used propaganda as a means of disseminating often misleading information to the German people that played on their fears and prejudices. Propaganda simply provided the Nazi Party a means of indoctrinating the German people with their belligerent ideology. The perpetrators of Nazi crimes were not indifferent bureaucrats following orders but fanatics that acted out of conviction that they were on the right side of history. For the Nazis, it was not about obedience but about conformity. When we choose a path of evil, we feel compelled to hide behind lies and clichés that give us a semblance of virtue. Humans are easily tempted by evil masquerading as good.

Paul Joseph Goebbels (1897–1945) was the Reich minister of propaganda in Nazi Germany from 1933 to 1945. He was recognised for his zealous oratory and anti-Semitism when he was appointed propaganda minister in 1933 alongside Hitler's rise to power. Goebbels exerted totalitarian control over the German media, arts, and information and used modern propaganda techniques to psychologically prepare the German people for war. His propaganda techniques were cynically contrived to achieve the desired results, with total disregard to the accuracy of the information. By openly exploiting the lowest instincts of the German people – racism, xenophobia, class envy, and insecurity – Goebbels freely acknowledged that he could play the popular will of the people, leading the masses wherever he wanted them to go. During World War II, Goebbels increased his power and influence to intensify the propaganda by urging the Germans to embrace the idea of total war. In the end, Goebbels and his family of six young children committed murder-suicide with Hitler in his Berlin bunker, which marked the end of the European war. Propaganda is still used by many governments today to maintain loyalty and provide a sense of calm and stability, particularly in times of crisis.

On the international stage, political leaders use bluffs as a means of unnerving their opponents. The Soviets were adept at pretending to have defence capabilities and arsenal that they did not actually possess, which kept the Americans highly anxious. When the Cold War finally ended in 1990, it was discovered that the deteriorating Soviet economy had failed to maintain the weapons, ships, submarines, and aircraft in full working order. Many of the nuclear submarines were found rusting in naval dockyards as they had fallen into disrepair, yet the Soviets were keen to hide their declining military strength behind a facade of exaggeration and puffery whilst the Cold War was in full swing. Americans also countered with their own bluff. The SDI or 'Star Wars' was a tactical bluff that Ronald Reagan used in the mid-1980s to jolt the Soviets into a new arms race that was unsustainable because of their dire economy. What the SDI did manage to do was to bring the Soviets rushing to the negotiating table. So in the game of international brinkmanship, lying or bluffing is an acceptable and commonly expected tactic that politicians use to deceive their opponents in an effort to avert the use of force. This tactic is precisely what Machiavelli prescribed in his famous book *The Prince*, when he stated to 'never . . . attempt to win by force what can be won by deception'.

CHAPTER 7

———

Avoid Regrettable Actions

Occasionally, politicians say or do things they come to regret. During the 2001 British electioneering campaign, the UK's deputy PM, John Prescott, started a fist fight with an onlooker who threw an egg at him in full view of the cameras. It became not only national news but also an international sensation that was screened all over the world. The deputy PM became known as the 'brawling minister', which did great harm to his reputation. He reacted under pressure and, in the process, could have easily destroyed his career. He was lucky and managed to salvage his reputation when the media came to his rescue with a straw poll that showed his actions were generally supported by the majority of 'white adult males'.

Politicians and leaders need to rise above the chaos and demonstrate prudence and resolve and not react in a way that exposes human weakness. It is perhaps better to ignore idiots than to fan their flames through a response that provides them with a wider audience, which Prescott could have done by not reacting the way he did. Hostile crowds or harsh media questioning can provoke emotional outbursts or negative comments that politicians may later regret, so calm restraint should always be the order of the day regardless of the circumstances. You must remember that tantrums neither intimidate nor inspire loyalty since a lack of self-control only creates doubts and uneasiness about your power.

The great motivational writer Napolean Hill once wrote, 'Think twice before you speak. Your words and influence will plant the seed of either success or failure in the mind of another.' As your position of influence and

———

87

power grows, people hang off every word you say, so it is essential to choose your words carefully since any wrong word that can be misconstrued can plant the seeds to your downfall. Treat all microphones as if they are live, even when the interview is finished because you may be caught off guard by conniving reporters who may say the interview is over but then ask you leading questions that trick you into comments that were never meant to be broadcast, like the instance when Australian reporter Mike Willesee came to the end of an interview with a senior gun lobbyist working for the NRA who let his guard down and confessed things about the underhanded tactics that the NRA use, thinking the cameras and microphones were off, which caused severe embarrassment.

Silly remarks may get you into a lot of hot water, so don't ever say anything that will come back to haunt you. Even a simple joke can reverberate into a national or, in Ronald Reagan's case, international crisis. Just before a radio interview, U.S. president Ronald Reagan jokingly stated he will give the order to commence nuclear attack on the Soviets. The live microphone picked up his comments, and the Soviets promptly went into high alert. Sometimes cameras can pick up body language or even lip-read what you say, so all public gatherings must be treated with care. If you are seated behind a visiting dignitary who is giving a speech and the cameras spot you snoozing away, the insult to the visitor will have immense repercussions on the diplomatic relations between your countries. All political leaders must mind their body language and choose their words carefully because inadvertent mishaps can easily be magnified in the public arena. Comments on social media must always be carefully crafted so that they cannot be used against you in a negative way. Even private emails can be hacked and expose delicate issues that could damage your profile, as it unfortunately happened to Hillary Clinton leading up to the 2016 U.S. presidential elections. Watch what you say, do, or write/text in the public domain because it can be used as ammunition by enemies who seek your downfall.

We are all emotional human beings, but political leaders need to put emotion into the back seat and think with clear heads. After all, human emotion is much stronger than reason when it comes to decisions, and there will be times when you will make mistakes. Don't try to justify or excuse your failures – own them! You can and will be wrong, but that is not a reflection of your weakness but a consequence of uncertainty. We improve only when we engage with our errors rather than deny them. In your political life, you'll be more respected and trusted by the people around you if you honestly own up to your mistakes. Learn from your mistakes and set an example that it's OK to get things wrong sometimes, especially when they are honest mistakes. The aviation industry rarely engages in blame and uses mistakes to drive learning because when pilots make mistakes, it results in their own deaths. When a politician makes a mistake, their life may be spared, but their decision may result in the death of thousands, as was the case during the 2020–2021 COVID-19 pandemic and ensuing global crisis that saw the preventable deaths of thousands of people in countries where the political leadership failed to provide proper guidance and advice to their citizens.

To safeguard their people, political leaders require good judgement, which depends on experience, keeping an open mind, and the willingness to accept new information. Being too fixated on knowing prevents you from ever finding out what you don't know. We learn more from people who challenge our thought processes than those who affirm our conclusions. Weak leaders respond to criticism by silencing their critics rather than taking it on board and accepting that perhaps something needs to change. It is important to remember that the man who believes he knows everything learns nothing. To improve the quality of our judgements, we need to overcome bias ('I know it all') as well as noise (distractions) such as our mood and fatigue, which may influence our decisions. Decisions should be based on their merits, not on status, so political leaders should not let their egos get in the way of making the best possible decision for the good of their people. After all, common sense is the knack of seeing things as they are and doing things as they ought to be done. A good leader must encourage a diversity of opinions to help generate better options, which are much more important than trying to make perfect decisions. When making an important decision, it is best to sleep on it and revisit it in the morning because sleep will give you a 30 per cent better chance of connecting the unconnected and getting a new idea or solving a difficult problem. Furthermore, political decisions should ultimately be based on your ability to sleep well at night.

Every day political leaders are confronted by intense media scrutiny and must field lots of questions, some of which are designed to trick politicians into saying things they were not meant to say. Questions that generate the greatest emotional response are a great indicator of challenging the way things are, which seasoned reporters are very good at. Never be tempted to respond to a question that entices you to criticise others, especially your own party colleagues. No matter how bad things appear, always project a sense of harmony and unity in your party and avoid airing your dirty laundry to the media. Everyone in your party must sing to the same tune, and those who stray must be quickly brought into line behind closed doors and not in full public view. When challenged with gruelling media questions, experienced politicians respond carefully and refuse to be pressured by reporters to give simple yes or no answers. Stalling tactics like 'This matter requires careful consideration' or 'I need to consult with my cabinet/department/party colleagues before I can respond to your question' may bide some time and provide a convenient escape route. A perennial favourite is 'I cannot comment until I have been fully briefed on the situation'. Deferring to others saves politicians from being pushed over the cliff by further, more penetrating questioning. It is not always the media you have to guard against, however. The devious tactics of opposition parties can also be quite onerous.

Seasoned leaders learn to refrain from answering every criticism levelled against them, particularly by opposition party members. In most situations, it may be best to begin with a dignified silence to purge the emotion from an immediate response and then reply with a succinct statement that is devoid of emotions or contentious details. If the attack gains momentum and begins to threaten your leadership, a judicious response is required to quell the uproar and restore the peace. Call a press conference and explain to the people what the issues are and what your party/administration/government intend to do about it. When faced with public demonstrations, political leaders should never be tempted or feel pressured to expose themselves in a public setting that could prove dangerous. An astute politician will never say or do anything that may inflame an already tense situation. Smiling and waving at angry crowds is like poking fun at a raging bull. If there is a public demonstration against your policies, avoid the temptation to address hostile crowds who are often not in the mood for reasoning. A ruler's safety is especially a major concern following riots that may be partly due to the result of high unemployment and poor economic conditions which their government has failed to address. Political leaders may understandably feel a need to visit the site of the riots, but the best course of action under these circumstances is to keep well away. Despite all good intentions, a visit by a politician may inflame the situation and spark further riots. There are times when political leaders are best to keep well away and avoid exposing themselves to an angry mob. It is much safer to make a public announcement from the safety of a television studio.

Political life at the top can be like a pressure cooker. The pressure to make hasty decisions can sometimes lead to ill-conceived responses. Sadly, for the people of Iraq, Saddam Hussein plunged his nation into turmoil through ill-conceived ideas and decisions that had the effect of throwing diplomacy out the window. Saddam Hussein (1937–2006) was president of Iraq from 16 July 1979 until 9 April 2003, when he was toppled by a coalition of Western nations led by the Americans in what became described as the second 'Gulf War'. A leading member of the revolutionary Ba'ath Party, which espoused a mix of Arab nationalism and socialism, Saddam rose to the position of general in the Iraqi armed forces and, by 1976, became the de facto leader of Iraq. He slowly began to consolidate his power over Iraq's government, and on 16 July 1979, he formally came to power when he forced the ailing al-Bakr, then president of Iraq, to resign.

Once in power, Saddam focused on achieving stability in a nation split along social, ethnic, and religious divisions, in particular Sunni versus Shi'ite Muslims. Saddam understood that political stability in a country divided into many factions required massive repression with the help of his paramilitary and police organisations. Saddam modernised the Iraqi economy and created a strong security apparatus to prevent coups and insurrections. With the help of increasing oil revenues, Saddam implemented a national infrastructure campaign by building roads, promoting mining, and developing other industries. Electricity was brought to nearly every city in Iraq and many outlying towns. Much as Adolf Hitler supported German industry in the 1930s, ending mass unemployment and building freeways (autobahns), Saddam had a clear understanding for what the Arab populace demanded, which earned him veneration abroad for his achievements. Unfortunately, Saddam's heavy-handed approach to foreign diplomacy with his immediate neighbours proved to be his undoing. The bloody eight-year Iran–Iraq War (1980–1988) ended in a stalemate. There were estimates of up to one million dead and hundreds of thousands of casualties during the bitter conflict, where both economies were left devastated. The end of the war with Iran precipitated latent tensions between Iraq and its wealthy neighbour Kuwait, who had loaned Iraq some \$30 billion to fight the futile war. When Saddam urged the Kuwaitis to forgive the Iraqi debt accumulated in the war, they refused.

Unexpectedly, the Kuwaiti refusal precipitated a cascade of events that resulted in the Iraqi invasion of Kuwait, which galvanised the international community to set up a coalition of armies that led to the first Gulf War in January 1991. Despite his resounding defeat, Saddam managed to cling on to power for another decade. However, his belligerent conduct in the face of mounting international pressure to disclose whether he had weapons of mass destruction eventually triggered a second Gulf War in 2003, when he was finally toppled from power. He ultimately met his ignominious fate by the hangman's noose in the final days of 2006.

Saddam has gone down in history as one of the last of the twentieth century's remorselessly cruel dictators, notable for unrelenting terror against his own people. His morbid will to power and capricious attacks on his own people created a pervasive fear in the population, who became complicit in his rule as the country became a nation of informants – friends on friends and communities on communities. His unprovoked attacks on Iran and Kuwait destabilised the Middle East and provoked a crisis, not only in the Arab world but also in the international community, who were compelled to intervene. It's no wonder his death was universally celebrated, not only by the international community but also by the Iraqi people themselves. Despite his early success in transforming Iraq from a fractured and backward nation to a modern society, he made bad decisions with respect to foreign policy, and his country suffered as a result. The pressure to resolve his nation's looming debt crisis with Kuwait using a heavy-handed approach sowed the seeds of his demise.

As Saddam Hussein clearly demonstrated, decisions made under pressure can have important consequences on your power and your political survival. A rapid decision made on the spur of the moment in a state of high confidence may likely result in a poor outcome. Often we simply make the best decision we can with the information we have and in the time that is available. Different politicians presented with the same information might make different decisions, often depending on how the information is framed and how much risk they are willing to tolerate. Most of our behaviour is habitual (fast thinking, intuition) rather than reasoned (slow thinking). In a fast-moving and uncertain world, the human brain has evolved to rely on quick decision-making tools. In situations of uncertainty, our decision making must rely on prediction. Therefore, for a political leader, it is crucial to think carefully and consult widely to avoid reacting under pressure and making poor decisions you come to regret.

After consulting with advisors, it is best to have a calm moment to yourself to reflect on the choices you have.

Politicians need to carefully consider all the repercussions of their actions as often their careers and ultimately their legacy may be doomed unless it can be salvaged by an overwhelming success that can repair the damage. A cleverly crafted speech, for instance, can have a deep and lasting impact on the political temperament of a nation that reverberates across the centuries, which will help neutralise some of your remorseful past actions. U.S. president Lincoln showed how a few carefully chosen sentences and phrases can truly change the mindset of a whole nation and, at the same time, overshadow some of the weaknesses he displayed prior to this moment. Following a two-hour oration by Edward Everett at Gettysburg, Pennsylvania, during the American Civil War on 19 November 1863, U.S. president Abraham Lincoln was invited to the podium to give a speech. In ten sentences which took just over two minutes to deliver, Lincoln presented what came to be regarded as one of the greatest speeches in American history. In the speech, he redefined the Civil War as the birth of a new freedom that will bring equality to all and create a unified nation. He ended his speech by exhorting the listeners to ensure the survival of America's representative democracy, that the 'government of the people, by the people, for the people, shall not perish from the earth'. Everett praised the president for his eloquent and succinct speech, saying, 'I should be glad if I could flatter myself that I came as near to the central idea of the occasion in two hours as you did in two minutes.' Incredibly, in the most understated response of the century, Lincoln replied that he was glad to know the speech was not a 'total failure'. The Gettysburg address, as it has now become known, is etched on a stone wall in the Lincoln memorial in Washington, D.C., as a lasting tribute to one of the greatest presidents in U.S. history. In just a few carefully crafted sentences, he encapsulated the history of the American Civil War and redefined the seeds of democracy for future generations to follow. Any weaknesses or regrettable actions he may have experienced during his lifetime were washed away by this one outstanding speech by which his presidency is defined. It seems success does forgive all sins.

Political leaders prone to hasty decisions that have not been carefully thought through can result in disastrous consequences as shown by Winston Churchill's decision in 1915 to open another front in the Dardanelles, which resulted in the catastrophic Gallipoli campaign that cost him his position as first lord of the admiralty and nearly destroyed his political career. Fortunately for Churchill, history remembers him more for his defiant stance against Nazi aggression and the saviour of his people in World War II than the disastrous decision that became the ANZAC legend of Gallipoli. So politicians must be very careful about their decisions, especially if made under pressure because the wrong decision can well be the last decision you ever make as a political leader.

Conviction is a good motive but a bad judge, so it is surprising how many political figures exhibit conviction as a sign of strength. Rational decisions cannot be made through the lens of emotions which are clouded by the hunger for power, attention, and glory. Often the emotional tail wags the rational dog, so that emotion is easily swayed by unrealistic expectations than by reason. The inability or unwillingness to separate emotion from reasoning often results in the denial of reality, which, in turn, may result in an action that you may regret. Sometimes politicians get caught in the trap of publicly stating their stance in the strongest possible way, only to find themselves publicly humiliated when they attempt to deny or retract what they said in the first place. Alas, once you make public your decision, you are obliged to stick by it; otherwise, people lose their faith and trust in you. That is why circumspection must always be factored into every decision before it is publicly announced. At the start of a political career, it is tempting to make a stand on every issue of the day. This gives the budding politician the conviction that they can be trusted. Unfortunately, a firm stance on any issue, especially if it goes on public record, can come back to haunt them in later years as they move up the ranks. Take, for example, contentious issues like abortion and assisted suicide. Once you go on the public record as backing one side or the other, unscrupulous enemies will dig up old files and use it against you, even years later, when you may have even made an about face on the issue. Australian PM John Howard, many years before he became PM, went on the public record with an anti-Asian immigration stance, which he later came to regret. His story is that of a survivor, which the title of his autobiography aptly acknowledged as *Lazarus Rising*.

John Winston Howard (1939–) was the second longest serving Australian PM after Sir Robert Menzies and the twenty-fifth PM of Australia (1996–2007). Howard represented the seat of Bennelong, New South Wales, as member of the House of Representatives from 1974 to 2007. He was federal treasurer (1977–1983) and leader of the opposition coalition parties from 1985 to 1989 and was re-elected as leader of the opposition in 1995 following the disastrous leaderships of Alexander Downer and John Hewson, the latter having lost the unlosable election to Labour's Paul Keating in 1993. Howard led the liberal-national coalition to victory at the 1996 federal election, ending a record thirteen years of coalition opposition. John Howard went on to lead three more election victories in 1998, 2001 and 2004, riding on the back of a period of strong economic growth and prosperity for Australia. During his eleven years as PM, Howard presided over major changes, including taxation, industrial relations, immigration, and Aboriginal relations. Despite his later success as PM, Howard made various statements in his early political career and took stands on issues that later came back to haunt him. In the 1960s, Howard supported Australia's involvement in the Vietnam War but, in later years, recognised his folly by admitting that his stand on the matter 'could have been handled and explained differently'. Howard was also averse to multiculturalism by suggesting that Asian immigration should be slowed to prevent social disorder. His stand on the issue of Asian immigration divided opinion, not only within his party but also amongst business leaders and intellectual opinion makers in the whole Asia-Pacific region, which many believe was instrumental in Howard subsequently losing the leadership of the opposition in 1989. In 1995 and again in 2002 as PM, Howard recanted his 1988 remarks on curbing Asian immigration.

He also stood firmly against Aboriginal land rights and refused to provide anything other than a personal apology to the 'stolen generation', which was capitalised on by the opposition Labour Party, who, under Kevin Rudd's subsequent leadership, reversed the awkward stand-off by making a formal apology broadcast throughout the nation. All the nation's political leaders were present during the momentous occasion – all except the former PM John Howard. On the economic front, Howard followed a protectionist and pro-regulation stance during his treasury years under Malcolm Fraser but reversed all these when he himself was PM almost two decades on. To avoid the disastrous election loss to Labour in 1993, Howard, as the newly re-elected opposition leader in 1995, revised his earlier statements against Medicare and considered that the Goods and Services Tax (GST) would 'never ever be part of coalition policy'. This ingeniously allowed Howard to turn the focus away from himself and on to Labour's recession of the early 1990s and the weary Labour government, which, in 1996, had been in power for thirteen years. This became known as the 'small target approach' to winning elections, which only Howard could implement with any success, as Labour leader Kim Beazley can attest to. Once in government, Howard promptly reversed his stance and introduced the GST. In 2007, despite undercurrents from his own party to step down in favour of the loyal deputy Peter Costello, Howard was determined to stay put as leader and not only lost the election but also lost his own parliamentary seat to an ex-news journalist with no political experience. It was an inglorious end to a political career that spanned four decades and produced the most celebrated survivor in modern political history thanks to his uncanny ability to resurrect his political fortunes with the determination and willpower that any lesser person would have struggled with. His ability to skilfully reverse his stance on many issues that would have otherwise buried his political fortunes remains legendary. He was acutely aware that a week is a long time in politics and that people have short memories, which he cleverly used to his advantage.

In the final years of John Howard's leadership, his loyal deputy and federal treasurer, Peter Costello, stood silently on the side lines as calls grew for Howard to step down in favour of Costello. What emerged was that just before Howard retook the leadership of the Liberal Party in 1995, he had made a verbal pact with Costello that he would eventually step down as PM for Costello, which, of course, never happened. A similar verbal agreement was alleged to have occurred a decade previously when PM Bob Hawke had promised the leadership to his faithful treasurer, Paul Keating. In the end, it was clear that once in power, Hawke was never going to let go, so Keating was forced to mount a hostile challenge, which he eventually won – but not without damaging their relationship for good. On the other side of the world, UK PM Tony Blair, it seems, made a similar pact with his fateful treasurer, Gordon Brown, who agreed not to challenge Blair for the Labour leadership if Blair agreed to step aside once Labour was comfortably in power in favour of Brown. Once again, Blair resisted all attempts to step down once in power until his position proved untenable and he was forced to resign.

So it seems that in their quest for power, politicians are prepared to say or do virtually anything that would facilitate their ascension to the top job, provided there is no record to prove either way. The only safe way to say something private and confidential is to meet face to face, in an isolated place, away from electronic devices. Once in power, leaders conveniently forget the promises and deals they made with loyal deputies who helped them to power. For the loyal deputies hoping that the verbal deals they made with their dear leaders all those years ago still stand, they are in for a rude awakening. What they sadly discover is that verbal agreement and pacts mean nothing and that leaders will never relinquish power based on what they had said to their colleagues years ago. If there is no written proof of the agreement, then it is clear that the agreements were only a means to an end for the leader involved, and that is to stop others from challenging them. What failed leadership aspirants fail to appreciate is that politics is a crafty game of out-manoeuvring your opponents by making promises you know will be quickly forgotten by all but the intended person it targets – and if a week is a very long time in politics, a year is an eternity!

Aspiring politicians need to ideally project an unblemished record so that political opponents have little or no ammunition they can use against them. However, as teenagers and young adults, we all tend to do silly things as part of growing up. Young people self-reveal before they self-reflect, which may haunt them with indiscretions from their past. Unfortunately, the early life of political leaders is fertile ground for scandal, and so a history of drug taking, sexual indiscretions, and breaking the law, no matter how trivial, may be resurrected and embellished by antagonists. A pertinent example of past indiscretions that nearly brought down a government was that of U.S. president Bill Clinton.

William Jefferson 'Bill' Clinton (born William Jefferson Blythe III on 19 August 1946) was the first U.S. president of the baby boomer generation and inaugurated at age forty-six. He was the third youngest president of the United States when he took office at the end of the Cold War in 1993. He served two terms as president before stepping down in 2001. He was a law graduate from Yale and had been governor of the state of Arkansas while still in his thirties, which was quite remarkable for a young man who grew up in a dysfunctional family with little but ambition to drive him. Clinton has been described as a 'New Democrat' who presided over the longest period of peacetime economic expansion in American history, with a budget surplus reported during the last three years of his presidency. In 1996, Clinton was re-elected and became the first Democrat since Franklin D. Roosevelt to win a second full term as president. Clinton finished his second and final term in office with the highest end-of-office approval rating of any U.S. president since World War II.

Based on what has just been described, you would be forgiven for thinking that Clinton had been a very successful president with an unblemished record. Unfortunately, his voracious sexual appetite and long history of sexual misdeeds dating back to his days as governor of Arkansas haunted his presidency, and he came very close to being thrown out of office. While he famously admitted to smoking cannabis at the university but claimed that he 'never inhaled', this paled to insignificance when, in front of a global media audience, he firmly denied having sexual relations with 'that woman'. That woman, of course, was Monica Lewinsky, a young and naive 22-year-old White House intern who ingratiated herself with the most powerful man in the world at the time. Occasionally, there are issues that are best left alone. If there is an issue you want buried, avoid discussing it, even with your closest friends. When Monica Lewinsky confided to a work associate, Linda Tripp, about her sexual encounters with U.S. president Bill Clinton at the White House, she never imagined that the co-worker would secretly record their telephone conversations regarding the affair with Clinton. Tripp then gave the recorded telephone conversations to Kenneth Starr, a lawyer who was investigating Clinton over the Whitewater controversy and the Paula Jones affair. To add further fuel to the fire, Linda Tripp managed to convince Monica Lewinsky to save all the gifts she had received from President Clinton and not to dry-clean the blue dress that had Clinton's sperm, which provided the evidence for the sexual encounter. This small indiscretion on Lewinsky's part snowballed into an international media frenzy which sent Lewinsky into hiding but did not spare the president, who had to face the world's media and deny any sexual encounters at a White House news conference on 26 January 1998. Unfortunately, a very determined Kenneth Starr decided to broaden his investigation to include the Lewinsky affair, which resulted in Clinton denying the sexual encounters while under oath. The encounter, which supposedly happened in the Oval Office, became a major scandal which led to Clinton's impeachment for perjury and obstruction of justice after he lied about his relationship with Lewinsky in a sworn deposition in the Paula Jones lawsuit, yet another sexual misconduct case that was dogging him at the time. What followed was public humiliation and impeachment for the president, who miraculously survived a narrow vote of confidence in the senate and went on to complete his second term of office.

It seems incredible that Clinton had his hands full trying to fend off sexual misconduct accusations while trying to run the country. Certainly, if Clinton lived in another era, none of this would have come to light. U.S.

president John F. Kennedy earned legendary status when it came to sexual dalliances in the White House, but it seems that the 1960s upheld the sacred mantra of 'don't ask and don't tell' – something that Clinton tried to introduce with gays in the armed forced some thirty years later. Despite his regrettable actions, Bill Clinton had a very down-to-earth demeanour and was liked by all, which undoubtedly saved his presidency. Discretion is paramount in political circles, but history has shown that many other political leaders are not so lucky.

Neutrality is another key political tactic you need to bolster your credentials. As you steadily climb the greasy pole of political power, do not let people drag you into their petty squabbles and fights but seem supportive and interested to both sides by remaining emotionally disengaged. Do not let yourself become the pawn for any cause but always remain impartial because only a sucker would rush to take sides. Let others brawl while you stand back, wait, and watch, while you grow more powerful with every conflict you avoid. You can make promises to both sides, but do not pledge yourself to any cause or side but yourself so that you become the kingpin that holds all the cards. As each side vies for your influence, you immediately become a person of great power and appeal. Once you step into a conflict that you did not choose to be part of, you lose your advantage. Every moment you waste on other people's affairs detracts from your own strength. Let other people exhaust themselves in conflict and then take advantage of their depleted energy. Remember that the only thing that matters is your own political survival, so it is in your best interests to stay neutral and rise above the internal factional squabbles so that you remain clean and ready to step into a power vacuum created by the conflict.

What we have learned from this chapter is that decisions need to be carefully thought out and not be influenced by emotional rhetoric, hostile criticism, or bad opinion polls. In other words, all decisions should be based on facts and not fanciful arguments by gifted orators or sponsored opinion polls. It is much worse to follow the wrong map than no map at all because overconfidence can be more harmful than confronting the reality that you're lost. The path taken should always meet the tripartite nexus of the maximum benefit, the least harm, and the collective good of your people. So in the case of territorial disputes with neighbouring countries, a diplomatic solution rather than military option should always take precedence because it is easy to start a war but very difficult to finish it. A decision should always be tempered with an escape clause that enables a quick change of mind if conditions or circumstances change. The adage of 'sticking to your guns' may sound tough and admirable, but in a complex world of constant change, a shrewd leader needs to be flexible enough to quickly adapt to changing circumstances as new facts emerge. Ultimately, you don't want to do or say something you may later regret.

CHAPTER 8

Plant the Seeds of Policies

A wise ruler knows that you never change things by fighting existing reality. In economic terms, people respond to incentives; when it becomes costly to do something, they will tend to do less and/or vice versa. If you raise prices, you lose market share. If taxes are too high, then people either stop working or find ways to avoid the formal economy through the black market. Plenty of well-intentioned government incentives, such as high taxes on the wealthy, end up being governed by the law of unintended consequences, such as offshore tax havens. Targeted tax increases end up lowering the projected tax intake as people are incentivised to avoid it. Before you decide to change things, pay attention to the value of what's already there because there is little chance of entering, let alone winning, the battle of ideas if the new model you are proposing is no better than the existing model you want to supplant. Governments cannot legislate behaviour without first considering people's natural desires and dreams. Therefore, a tax system that specifically incentivises the things we want and reduces the things we don't want is the ideal way to collect it. Like Al Gore once said, 'let's tax what you burn rather than what you earn', which most people can relate to and agree with, which makes it easier to enact.

Politicians who enact rules and legislative laws do so based on their own position in society (i.e. their gender, race, sexual orientation, religion, culture, etc.). So the rules enacted by politicians of the day are essentially driven by paternalistic conviction that they know what's best for others, and that knowledge and authority vested in their position gives them the right to regulate and control others' behaviour, whether they like it or not. Soft paternalism seeks to influence or nudge the decision making of others but stops short of prohibition, which is what most liberal nations strive for. Hard paternalism simply bans the things that governments do not like, which is characteristic of theocracies like Iran and Afghanistan and communist nations like China and North Korea. What seems unethical and even immoral today might seem quite ordinary and mundane in the future. Homosexuality was a crime up until recent years, and same-sex marriage was unheard of until now. Therefore, it is not surprising that many of our policy mistakes of the past were errors of fact based on defective thinking and on the erroneous assumptions that we make about other people at the time of legislation. A good political leader needs to be forward thinking when it comes to policy ideas that will survive the test of time.

Australia's remarkable transformation from a homogenous white British outpost still reliant on the motherland to an independent multifaceted nation composed of different cultures, beliefs, and ideologies was a product of policies developed by politicians whose collective vision made Australia what it is today. As distinct from protocol or law, a policy guides decisions or actions that achieve desired outcomes, and unlike the law, a policy cannot compel or prohibit behaviours, like the compulsory wearing of helmets by motorcyclists. In the decision-making process, policies are considered a form of commitment, so the political party that develops the policy is also held accountable for the policy. Examples of policy include parliamentary rules of order and presidential executive orders if you're American. As a statement of intent, a policy directs important political decisions for programmes or spending priorities which focus on explicit goals that are considered by the political party to generate the most popular public support, such as building more prisons to counter the high crime rate.

What is the difference between good and bad policy? Bad policies are those that interfere with national growth by setting up barriers which increase costs, over-regulate the economy (which stifles new business), and eliminate incentives for the disadvantaged of society to help themselves. Good policies are those that encourage competition, devise incentives that attract new business, and eliminate barriers and regulations that stymie the growth of the national economy. If the imperious communist system taught us anything, it is that the absence of an effective opposition eliminates the government's obligations to meet the needs of its people. A simple rule of thumb is that the government should not be the sole provider of a service unless, according to economist Charles Wheelan, there are compelling reasons to believe that the private sector will fail in that role. Social welfare, public health, and national defence are some of the many responsibilities that only the government can administer. History has shown, however, that government-run power stations, banks, hotels, telecommunications, and public transport stifle any need to be innovative or responsive to customers, which makes everybody worse off. As one big government monopoly, the benefits of competition are lost, and customer service becomes a byword for 'wait your turn'.

The role of opposition is to counter government control by scrutinising and arguing for better policies so that voters can appreciate that there is a credible choice in an alternative government. Essentially, the opposition is required to hold the government to account. Condemning bad policy is the most effective weapon in the opposition's arsenal. The key to effective opposition is the ability to target and pull apart bad policy without humiliating individual ministers by mudslinging and personal tirades. Personal attacks reflect a regressive behaviour that few members of the public would condone in politicians. Public spats among politicians give the impression of schoolyard bullying that only fuels public antipathy. People know when a minister has made a blunder, and the opposition merely needs to underscore the blunder. The ability to develop, defend, and appraise policy is an essential tool of a competent government minister. In a parliamentary debate, the side with the most convincing arguments always wins, regardless of the truth. Politicians, like lawyers, always cherry-pick the evidence that will bolster their case and ignore inconvenient truths which threaten their defence. Rising junior politicians must avoid personality conflicts and concentrate on policy debate, which is the springboard they need to further their career aspirations. Their performance in the public arena on policy issues not only provides valuable experience for future leadership roles but also may act as the impetus for promotion. Public hostility towards your opponents only damages your own reputation.

One of the worst instances of personal hostilities in Australian parliamentary history was during the government of PM Paul Keating (1991–1996). As Keating was a parliamentary performer, his scathing criticisms and personal attacks on the opposition were legendary and rather disconcerting for the public. He personified the 'bully politician', ready to lash out with tirades and personal insults that sat uncomfortably with the Australian public. While his performance was at times entertaining, it added little to the political debate and often belittled the issues at hand when criticism was directed at the opponent rather than the policy. His personal standing suffered considerably from his lizard-like tongue, and by 1996, the Australian public had had enough and were ready for a change of leadership, which gave John Winston Howard the belated opportunity to secure the top job. John Howard may have lacked the character and personality of Paul Keating, but he went on to become the second longest serving PM in Australia's history – a great consolation, no doubt, for having endured and survived the verbal lashings of his predecessor while in opposition. So focusing on policies rather than personalities is essential to political success.

A rational and methodical attack on bad policy is the key to undermining the confidence of government initiatives. Take the example of illegal asylum seekers. The mandatory detention of illegal refugees was John Howard's answer to stopping boatloads of asylum seekers arriving on Australian shores. His reasoning was based on a simple message: that we (Australians) should decide who comes to our shores and not the criminal people smugglers. The simple message struck a positive chord with the Australian people, which made it more acceptable when the boat arrivals did dramatically decrease as a result of the policy. The opposition's attempts to attack the policy failed as their arguments were based on ideology (i.e. innocent people should not be incarcerated) but they had no credible alternative policies that would stop the boat arrivals. No sooner had John Howard and his coalition government been voted out of office in 2007 than the illegal boatloads of asylum seekers returned in their droves as the newly elected Labour government had no alternative policies on how to manage the boatloads of illegal refugees. The lesson in this story is that if you attack government policy, make sure your party has credible and practical alternatives because once you're in government, you may be forced to adopt the same policies as your predecessor. Hypocrisy and public support do not make good bedfellows.

While personal attacks are generally damaging in modern politics, there are rare occasions where skilful politicians can employ subtle strikes to enhance their personal standing in public opinion polls. One such example was during the second U.S. presidential debate in 1984 when the

74-year-old incumbent president Ronald Reagan confronted questions about his age and responded, 'I will not make age an issue of this campaign. I am not going to exploit, for political purposes, my opponent's youth and inexperience,' which generated applause and laughter, even from his opponent Walter Mondale himself, who lost the presidential race to the White House. This was a clever tactic that totally disarmed the opponent in an entertaining way that avoided ugly personal attacks and neutralised the 'age' issue in Reagan's favour. While it takes great skill and experience to disarm opponents and neutralise arguments, it also takes a very stoic and disciplined politician to stay focused on the issues at times when a heated debate threatens to degenerate into a mudslinging contest. Occasionally, television news programmes gleefully show members of parliament of some foreign country engaged in an all-out brawl reminiscent of the American Wild West. I'd imagine it would not be a very pleasing sight for citizens to see their politicians in a taxpayer-funded wrestling extravaganza.

Leaders need to rise above the personal bickering and focus on issues rather than personalities. There is no need to respond to personal insults with further personal insults; otherwise, the debate degenerates into a bunfight, and important issues take a back seat as politicians slug it out. The cordial relationship between Australian PM John Howard and the Labour opposition leader Kim Beazley in the late 1990s was an exceptional example of professional politicians getting on with the job of parliamentary debate. The mutual respect between the two leaders ensured that policies remained the top priority, with good policies gaining bipartisan support and bad policies attracting healthy debate. The PM is the people's representative, and any disrespect towards the PM is an affront to the people he represents. Calling the PM an 'egghead' on national television, for example, demonstrates a clear disrespect for Australian government institutions and the Australian people. Politicians who engage in public mudslinging run the risk of being repudiated by the voting public and renounced by their own political party.

Seasoned politicians are always careful not to criticise individuals and refer collectively to the government or opposition or minor party when commenting on issues. This is not always the case, however, especially in some countries where personal attacks form the very fabric of political life. The government of Venezuela is a typical example of strong personalities taking precedence over good governance. The late Hugo Rafael Chávez Frías (1954–2013) was president of Venezuela until his death while still in office in 2013. He was a firm anti-imperialist and vocal critic of neoliberal capitalism. From the time he became president in 1999, Chávez was a vocal opponent of the United States' foreign policy and strongly allied himself with the socialist governments of Cuba, Bolivia, and Ecuador, which is seen as a part of the leftist 'pink tide' sweeping Latin America. Chávez was a divisive and highly controversial figure both at home and abroad, and according to his biographers, he earned his place in history as the president most loved and most despised by the Venezuelan people. His opponents, particularly those of the middle and elite classes, often accused him as being vulgar and common. His supporters were mainly poor, young, politically unsophisticated, and undemocratic masses who are armed, controlled, and funded by the state, which partly explains the high crime rate still ravaging the country. The racist term 'ese mono' or 'that monkey' was commonly used by opponents to describe Chávez, which reflected the enormity of his unpopularity with upper classes who saw his left-leaning policies as a threat to their lifestyles and wealth. Obviously, Venezuela is a nation where personal attacks are an acceptable and integral part of their political system and so are tolerated rather than condemned. Policy debate often took a back seat when Hugo and his cronies fended off criticism by countering with personal attacks.

Like Venezuela, many of the developing nations seem to focus on personalities and forget or simply ignore that policies should be guiding the political process. The worst governments are effectively policy neutral and spend their parliamentary debates attacking one another while the country flounders in a sea of uncertainty. That is why prosperous nations spend millions of dollars on policy development which are handled by many university departments devoted to public policy, especially in Western Europe and the United States. Prosperous countries are blessed with visionary politicians who have policies that serve in the best interests of the nation. Sadly, many developing nations suffer economic hardships, famine, and civil war because their political leaders have failed in their duties to formulate credible policies. Poor governance results from poor policies which give rise to failed states. That is the fundamental difference between rich and poor nations.

In the private sector, resources are allocated where there are profits to be made. Conversely, the government allocates resources according to wherever the political process takes them. In other words, where the private sector is driven by profits, the government is driven by votes, and votes at the ballot box are ultimately determined by policies. As smartphones continue to morph into personal information hubs, they will become the basis for big data collection about our behaviour, where we eat, work, and play, how we travel, and whom we interact with. It will become the government's much-needed nervous system so that policies are based on fact rather than guesswork. Knowing the typical behaviour patterns in a community can allow governments to better plan transportation, community services, and growth. In a fundamental sense, policies are the hard currency used by political parties to garner votes. Political parties are appraised at election time according to the political agenda and policies they bring to the electorate. Agendas and policies that strike a chord with the voting public, such as harsher penalties for domestic violence, can help generate popular support. So if you want to set a new political agenda, you first need to plant the seed and watch it grow.

On the eve of the 2011 Australian Formula 1 Grand Prix, the Lord Mayor of Melbourne, Robert Doyle, made a comment that shook the very foundations of the sport. He simply asked the question whether the F1 international motor race was worth the $50 million of subsidies from taxpayers. As predicted, there was an uproar from all those who had a vested interest in the sport. In the weeks leading up to the 2011 event, a trickle at first, followed by a tide of dissent, began to emerge about whether the F1 Grand Prix was, in fact, worth the money the state government had to pour into it to keep it viable. What Robert Doyle did is that he carefully planted the seed and watched it grow into its own. With a simple question, he achieved what he set out to do, and that is to plant the seeds of doubt and dissent that snowballed into an avalanche of concern and protest which those in the higher echelons of power could not ignore. Sometimes it is better to keep your message simple and to the point, and if it strikes a chord with the people, the issue will gather its own momentum.

The above example of the Formula 1 Grand Prix was a leading question that was cleverly designed to provoke a negative response. If Robert Doyle was looking for a positive response, then he may have conveniently ignored the $50 million cost to taxpayers and asked whether the estimated $30 million that the motor event brings to the city is even more reason to keep the race firmly on the Melbourne calendar. The response, I'm sure, would have been very different. Politicians are very skilful at filtering information and cherry-picking statistics or facts that serve their own agenda.

Small everyday actions have spill-over effects on the actions of others.

Each action we take affects those around us in a ripple effect that may extend beyond our immediate social circle. When you plant a seed of a big idea amongst your followers, you hope that a tree will grow and bear fruit. Gardeners don't make plants grow, but they do create conditions where plants can thrive. In political terms, planting a seed is all about setting a political agenda which subscribes to a set of issues and policies that make news and stimulate discussion. Political agendas can sometimes be shaped or influenced by media personalities (e.g. Jamie Oliver, school dinners), grass-roots activists (e.g. the IRA), and non-government organisations such as Greenpeace, a worldwide non-governmental environmental organisation with a stated goal to 'ensure the ability of the Earth to nurture life in all its diversity'. Greenpeace focuses on global issues such as deforestation, commercial whaling, anti-nuclear issues, and global warming. It started as the Don't Make a Wave Committee, which sent a chartered ship from Vancouver to Amchitka, Alaska, to protest the testing of nuclear devices by the United States in September 1971. It subsequently changed its name to Greenpeace and has evolved into the largest and most visible environmental organisation in the world. Its high-profile campaigns against toxic waste and commercial whaling make news headlines around the world. The activities of Greenpeace are deliberately designed for maximum publicity to not only generate public awareness of environmental issues but also, more importantly, influence the political agenda so that governments are pressured to sit up and take notice. The direct action taken by Greenpeace on many environmental issues often makes news headlines and sows the seeds for change.

Experienced politicians know that we are shaped and influenced by those around us. Our desires and preferences are largely based on what our peers find acceptable rather than on rational reflection. Most of our public beliefs and habits are learned by observing the attitudes, actions, and outcomes of peers rather than by logic and reasoning. The dynamics of a group usually exert pressure on us to conform so that people who have similar opinions are probably under social pressure to hold the same opinions. Group pressure can cause us to ignore what we can plainly see with our own eyes because the infectious belief of the group overwhelms the sceptical individual. The larger the group of followers is, the easier they are to deceive because people in large groups are more emotional and less able to reason and doubt. In a group, we become actors, moulding what we say and do so that others accept and like us and see us as loyal team members. In a larger group setting, we might be led to say or do things we would never have said or done on our own. Far more people are willing to step up if you ask them to do something big than if you ask them to do something small. Likewise, people within a political movement constantly reinforce one another's beliefs in a self-perpetuating loop. That is why successful politicians cleverly target key opinion leaders when it comes to garnering votes.

The political leader who speaks in unshakeable certainties will gain a larger following than a responsible leader who speaks in probabilities. They emphasise enthusiasm over rationality and clear thinking. They promise something great and transformative which they keep vague and simple but full of hope. A combination of vague promises, alluring concepts, and burning enthusiasm will stir people's thoughts because most people want to hear that a simple solution will address all their problems. Humans have a desperate need to believe in something, anything, which makes them gullible; hence, they manufacture faiths out of nothing and follow con artists and charlatans who become their object of worship. When we are filled with fear or doubt, we tend to follow the crowd. People in a crowd are highly suggestable, and people can feel relieved of any personal responsibility by deferring to their ruler. As a ruler, you cannot effectively organise masses of people if you stick to pure reality without mixing any fiction or fantasy with it. Narratives always make more sense than reality because people prefer simple explanations, which is why we are inclined to believe in myths, legends, and conspiracy theories.

People's attention is easily swayed by hearsay, and cunning politicians know how to exploit this phenomenon. For example, sowing rumours and poking holes in their reputation, political rivals become infuriated and unsettled to the point of making mistakes. Once the rumours stick, you stand aside and let public opinion hang them. It is well understood that all it takes is one bad misadventure to completely overturn ten good deeds because people tend to focus on the bad. Planting rumours of misdeeds can do a lot of damage to your opponent's standing because few ever bother to check the facts since a good story does not rely on the truth. In fact, even if the rumour proves to be false, the retraction will have nowhere near the same impact as the rumour itself.

Vested interest groups appeal to people's emotions, instincts, and prejudices to gain favour, which is how the general public can be easily manipulated to believe whatever you want them to believe. Wily politicians and narrow interest pressure groups exploit this instinct to either sow seeds of doubt or encourage fidelity. The main casualty is the truth. In 1978, fluoride was introduced to Melbourne's water supplies after two decades of thorough dental scientific research showed the clear benefits of water fluoridation in dramatically decreasing the dental decay experience in children's teeth. As a disease prevention measure, it was an outstanding success, and the long-term safety of water fluoridation was proven beyond reasonable doubt. The local dental profession quickly witnessed a substantial drop in dental decay in their patients across the board, and leading dental organisations embraced the policy of water fluoridation wholeheartedly.

Following the success of the Melbourne water fluoridation programme, the state government attempted to roll out the scheme to regional cities and country towns but came up against fierce resistance from local communities. It transpired that a small but vocal group of anti-fluoridation activists had already contacted community leaders in regional cities and towns and planted the seeds of doubt with emotive terms like 'poison', 'mass medication', 'denial of freedom to choose', and so on before the dental profession and the government had their chance to explain the science and real benefits behind the scheme. The disturbing impact that the anti-fluoridation activists had on the emotions, fears, and prejudices of the people of the small towns and regional centres throughout Victoria delayed the introduction of water fluoridation for many years. The sad reality is that activists clearly know how to press all the right emotional buttons to get their message across, while scientists struggle to win the hearts and minds of the public simply because when they bypass the heart, they find the mind closed for business.

While we cannot predict the future, we can ensure that the foundations we lay today will support the right choices, whatever they may be. When it comes to decisions, human emotions are more powerful than rational thought, and this is precisely what astute politicians exploit when it comes to setting political agendas. Data can be manipulated to support any argument, which clever politicians can easily exploit to their advantage. The contentious issue of illegal refugees arriving on boats in Australian waters, which we have previously mentioned, has been in the public radar for many years now. On the one hand, right-leaning politicians merely put out statements to the effect that 'illegal refugees should be turned back'. This approach does little to set the agenda, and clearly, few people would take notice of such an unconstructive comment. Alternatively, a more effective approach would be to ask a leading question: 'Should illegal refugees, who bypass the normal visa process, be turned away?' Clearly, from the wording of the question, it appears to be seeking an affirmative response – yes, illegal refugees are bad – which many people will happily subscribe to. However, if the question was rephrased by a Greens senator – 'Should refugees, fleeing persecution, be turned back to face the possibility of death?' – the public's response would be very different. Ideally, when polling takes place, the questions posed should be worded in a way that elicits accurate information on the topic of interest because survey results can be extremely sensitive to the way a question is worded or framed. In public opinion polls, the phrasing of the question and the choice of language can matter enormously. Politicians try to manipulate voters' responses by choosing emotive words or language that can skew the responses. That is why opinion polls commissioned by different political organisations are virtually meaningless because the questions are loaded to provide the very answers that the parties seek to justify their stance on the issues. It's common knowledge in the political world that you never begin an inquiry or commission a public poll unless you already know the outcome. Similarly, when setting the agenda, only ask the questions that provide you with the answers you want.

In setting the political agenda, political leaders must first go to the people with the seeds of an idea and explain its virtues. The best way to explain anything is to use simple language that focuses on what's most important and leave out what's least important. It is only when the people can see that the idea has important repercussions that can change their own lives that they will respond. As an example, let's take another look at the time when the Australian government wanted to establish a carbon tax. The focus was on the negative impact of pollution and greenhouse gases so that the public were enticed to come on board with solutions to tackle climate change. Taking the time to explain the connection between carbon-based pollution and poor health creates a positive desire for people to support measures that reduce carbon-based pollution. People do not look at ideology; they only see policies in terms of how they affect them and their way of life. Few people care about melting polar icecaps and its effect on polar bears, but plenty care about the cost of electricity. Political leaders need to be able to effectively respond to the public concern of 'What's in it for me?' If the response is that a carbon tax will save the environment but will increase your power bills, then most people will baulk. However, if the carbon tax helps reduce asthma levels in children, then this becomes a more compelling argument than some vague idea that sea levels may rise in fifty years. By emphasising the real and immediate dangers of carbon-based pollution on the health and welfare of Australia's children, then people may be more inclined to accept the added cost of a cleaner environment. Shrewd political leaders must present arguments that people can relate to at the most fundamental level. The vague notion that sea levels may rise in fifty years will not bring on a stampede of concerned citizens to the steps of parliament urging the government to bring on a carbon tax. However, the prospect of an immediate and significant increase in power bills with the carbon tax will have people rioting on the streets to kill off any idea of a carbon tax that will lead to a rise in the cost of living.

Governments harbour the misconception that the general public cannot be trusted to understand what is good for them, and so they ignore the public at their peril when it comes to formulating policy. Most political commentators would agree that it is a brave political leader who makes the effort to engage public debate on contentious issues. However, it takes an exceptionally astute politician to plant the right seeds that will guide the debate in their favour. Planting the right seeds in people's minds activates a process that politicians can exploit to achieve the desired outcomes. Just like the activists who push all the right emotional buttons to get their message across, politicians need to understand the fears, prejudices, and aspirations of the public to plant their simple message and watch it grow. Your message needs to be simple if it is going to appeal to the masses. If you want people to follow you, give them the seeds of an idea they understand and can connect with. Begin by asking a question or making a statement that most people will agree with, and thereafter, you've got their attention.

CHAPTER 9

Understanding Leadership

Power and fame are like aphrodisiacs which are equally destructive in their relationship to the common man. Ambition for status and power fuels a sense of entitlement, which is a dangerous proposition for any organisation which harbours such leaders. Being treated like a VIP corrupts the social attitudes of the person who expects to live above the rules that govern the common man. Bad leadership thrives on arrogance and entitlement, and such a person who is hellbent on power is like a hopeless drug addict who will lie, steal, cheat, and commit acts of violence to get their next fix or, in the leader's case, to hold onto power. Granting someone too much power can sometimes turn normal talented people into unreasonable, irrational people who lose their sense of the real world and become obsessed with their own. They become destructive of themselves and of others. Excessive power leads to the temptation to take advantage of and to treat other people like suckers, which becomes an irresistible temptation as time in office grows. Ambitious people addicted to the pursuit of power, status, or fame are rarely satisfied and openly demonstrate unashamed greed for more. With power comes some of the greatest and most dangerous delusions, entitlement, control, and paranoia. Each conquest only whets their appetite for more. Hitler's dream of world domination fuelled the expansion of Nazi Germany into most of Europe until reality put a stop to his inflated imagination.

Where most leaders would have capitulated to Hitler, Churchill made it clear that he would fight on. Where others would have looked at the hopeless situation for Britain during the dark years of World War II, Winston Churchill saw hope in the shape of America. His vision for Britain was that of liberty, not subservience. Churchill saw things that others could not see, and that is victory through perseverance and alliance. Even in the darkest hours, he never gave up hope and rallied his nation to go on despite the relentless bombing and enemy attacks.

Winston Leonard Spencer-Churchill (1874–1965) was one of the great wartime leaders and served as UK PM twice (1940–1945 and 1951–1955). He is best remembered for his leadership of Britain during the darkest times of the Second World War. Widely regarded as an eminent statesman and renowned orator, Churchill was also a historian, a writer, an artist, and an officer in the British Army. During his long life, he received many honours and awards. Churchill was born into aristocracy as a descendent of the Dukes of Marlborough. His father, Lord Randolph Churchill, served as chancellor of the exchequer in the late nineteenth century and was regarded as a charismatic politician. His mother, Jenny Jerome, was an American socialite who married into British society and was instrumental in Churchill's early career through her many contacts in high places. When he was a young army officer, Jenny helped Winston secure passage as a war correspondent to various military theatres of action, such as in British India, the Sudan, and the Second Boer War, where he gained fame through newspaper articles and books he wrote about his campaigns.

For more than fifty years, Churchill held many political and cabinet positions and was constantly at the forefront of politics. Unfortunately, his political career was not all smooth sailing. During the First World War, he was first lord of the admiralty when he initiated and sponsored the disastrous Gallipoli campaign, which resulted in his shameful departure from government. Churchill's opposition to home rule for India and his resistance to the 1936 abdication of Edward VIII also created further controversies which kept him out of office and politically 'in the wilderness' during the 1930s. During this time, Churchill vigorously campaigned for the rearmament of British forces as the dark clouds of war loomed with Hitler's ascent to absolute power in Germany; Churchill's was the lone voice crying out about the danger from Hitler's resurgent Germany, but his warnings had gone largely unheeded. It was, therefore, no surprise that Churchill was recalled to the admiralty as the first lord upon the outbreak of World War II. Churchill fiercely criticised Neville Chamberlain's appeasement of Adolf Hitler, and in a speech to the House of Commons, he prophetically stated, 'You were given the choice between war and dishonour. You chose dishonour, and you will have war.'

It was not long before Churchill finally became PM following the resignation of Neville Chamberlain on 10 May 1940, when Britain stood alone in its active defiance of Hitler. His first speech as PM was the famous 'I have nothing to offer but blood, toil, tears, and sweat'. His steadfast leadership and dogged refusal to consider defeat helped inspire British resistance, especially during the difficult early days of the war. Early in the war, there was little good news to offer the British people, so he deliberately emphasised the dangers instead. Churchill refused to consider an armistice with Hitler's Germany, which encouraged resistance and hardened public opinion against a peaceful resolution as he prepared the British public for a long and protracted fight. Churchill's memorable speeches and radio broadcasts helped rouse the British people to reject surrender and fight on to the bitter end. Just before the Battle of Britain, he gave a rousing speech which included the following famous passage:

> We shall fight with growing confidence and growing strength in the air. We shall defend our island, whatever the cost may be. We shall fight on the beaches. We shall fight on the landing grounds. We shall fight in the fields and in the streets. We shall fight in the hills. We shall never surrender.

As the Battle of Britain gathered pace, he once again provided hope with the following words:

> Let us therefore brace ourselves to our duties and so bear ourselves that if the British Empire and its Commonwealth last for a thousand years, men will still say, 'This was their finest hour.'

In August 1940, as the Battle of Britain raged on overhead, Churchill emerged from an underground bunker and spoke one of his most famous lines: 'Never in the field of human conflict was so much owed by so many to so few', 'the few' referring to the brave RAF fighter pilots who went on to win the battle that nearly brought Britain to its knees.

Despite many setbacks, including numerous personal health scares, Churchill led Britain to a glorious victory over Nazi Germany. After the Conservative Party's surprise loss at the 1945 election, Churchill stayed on as leader of the opposition until 1951, when he again became PM, before retiring under pressure from his own party in 1955. When he died in 1965, he was given a state funeral, which saw one of the greatest assemblies of world statesmen ever. Churchill is widely regarded as amongst the most influential men in British history. Whilst Churchill was a flawed individual who made many poor decisions that delayed his ascent to power, he had a fighting spirit and an uncanny way of connecting with the man on the street through the most powerful words and phrases ever used in the English language. His ability to mobilise a whole nation behind him with stirring speeches that had immediate and profound impact on all those subsumed by the war made him a hero and a great wartime leader whose legacy lives on in the annals of notable historical figures of the twentieth century. It took a major global crisis to bring out the best in Churchill, and it seemed that the war was just what Churchill needed to fulfil his greatest political ambitions. While we all think that it is political leaders who shape events, sometimes it is the events that shape political leaders. Strangely, if World War II had never eventuated, Winston Churchill would have been but a footnote in history.

For leaders to get their message across, like Churchill did, they need a narrative that speaks to millions of ordinary people. Stories or narratives are ways in which political leaders try to make sense of complex situations for the benefit of their followers. When trying to explain something, it is best to come up with a positive and memorable story because well-told stories are emotional, and people remember stories rather than numbers and graphs. Stories of individual examples are better retained by audiences than cold logic or broad statements. Storytelling can draw in listeners and get them to act in ways that they would not have acted had they been presented with just the facts, for nothing sells better than a good story. Listeners absorbed in a story drop their guard and become more willing to accept arguments uncritically. That is why successful politicians build an emotional connection with their followers – so they lose track of rational considerations and yield to their agenda. Some narratives are contagious because they seem to confirm existing opinions or familiar beliefs, whereas narratives that seem contrary to prevailing thought often fail to go viral. Audiences do not respond well to things that are new or different, which stems from the deep fear of change and the uncertainty it could bring. People avoid change because it means venturing out of their comfort zone, especially if you can't connect the dots for them in a convincing way.

The greatest leaders are those who challenged the status quo and brought about sweeping changes that improved the lot of their people. Leaders who effectively drive change are those who patiently wait for the right moment because ideas, however extreme, can change the world only when the time is right. Instead of changing people's minds, you can appeal to values and beliefs that they already hold. Therefore, to sell a new idea, it must be wrapped in something that people already know. It is much easier for people to accept familiar ideas than totally original ones because if the ideas are too original, then it may be too hard for the audience to accept or understand them. Essentially, the goal is to push the envelope, not to tear the envelope. Radical ideas are best presented in a way that is less shocking and more appealing to mainstream audiences by planting the seeds of a simple idea before revealing the larger idea.

People with strong leadership characters are open to new ideas and ways of doing things. Good leadership depends on the ability to motivate and inspire others through optimism and pragmatic enthusiasm for what can be achieved. Effective leaders imbue themselves with an air of complete confidence and optimism, which infects their followers' spirits. Intelligent leaders surround themselves with talented people who are motivated to succeed by empowering them to choose the best ways to achieve a shared goal. Charismatic leaders circulate actively through a workplace and engage people in short, high-energy conversations, asking what is happening in people's lives and how their projects are doing, which makes everyone feel good – rather like bees harvesting pollen from many flowers, they develop a good sense of everything that is going on.

Progressive nations place a limited tenure on their leaders, which means that leadership is mostly a temporary custodianship of pivotal responsibilities. The legacy of good leadership isn't about being indispensable; it's about helping others be prepared to possibly step into your shoes. Succession planning is key to the long-term survival of any organisation, but when a leader is appointed for life, that's when things start to go bad. Unfortunately, history is replete with examples of bad leaders who plundered their nation's wealth for their own personal gains, but it's not just greed and selfishness that defines bad leaders. Leaders with questionable integrity who accept anything that is illegal, immoral, or unethical quickly lose the respect of their followers and end up harming the reputation of high office. Indecision and adversity to risk are two other traits that declare themselves as weak and ineffectual leadership qualities. A weak person is a reactive individual whose character and attitudes are moulded by others. Someone who stands for nothing or everything or safe things will leave no legacy. However, the most insidious of all the bad leadership qualities is the fear of change, which stifles progress and smothers development, to the detriment of the whole nation. China and India are two classic examples where inward-looking leadership, afraid of change from outside influences, failed to provide any material improvement in the lives of their people. It was only when the leadership of both nations accepted change as inevitable and opened their markets to global trade that the standard of living for their citizens was raised exponentially. Having accepted and adapted to change as a necessary part of progress, China has become the economic powerhouse of the twenty-first century, thanks largely to the visionary reforms of its diminutive leader Deng Xiaoping.

Deng Xiaoping (1904–1997) was leader of the Communist Party of China and a reformer who led China towards a market economy. Deng served as the leader of China from 1978 to 1992 after inheriting a country fraught with social and institutional calamities resulting from the Cultural Revolution of the Mao era. Despite his age and his involvement in the communist revolution in 1949, Deng represented the new generation of Chinese leadership and was considered the architect of a new style of socialism with Chinese characteristics. Deng embraced the socialist market economy as the basis for Chinese economic reform that opened China to foreign investment, the global market, and private competition. Deng is credited with raising the standard of living of hundreds of millions of Chinese by developing China into one of the fastest growing economies in the world. China is now the largest economy, second only to the United States.

A strategy that lacks the ability to exploit opportunity will not win because part of being a successful politician is being opportunistic, which involves waiting for the right circumstances to present themselves. Political leaders who are flexible and versatile are better able to change their strategies to capitalise on new opportunities. Your instinct should always be to say yes to every opportunity that presents itself, for you may never get another chance. Unexpected challenges bring opportunities which good leaders will exploit and bad leaders will shun. In a crisis, a competent leader will see beyond the immediate situation and think outside the square, which makes all the difference between victory and defeat. Bad leaders feel trapped in a bubble and rely too much on existing protocols to get them through, but good leaders see beyond their immediate surroundings and find solutions outside the box they live in. Good leadership is one that looks beyond the confines of today and sees a future that others cannot envision because they have their heads in the sand. The ability to see the situation from the outside allows a good leader to prescribe effective measures from the inside because a grand vision is a key element of good leadership.

Leadership can come in many guises. A transactional leader is one who adapts and responds to the changing circumstances and events. U.S. president Roosevelt was one such leader who, prior to the Japanese attack on Pearl Harbor, promised that Americans will not fight in any foreign wars. Immediately after Pearl Harbor, he mobilised the whole nation into a war effort that focused on not only Japan but also the European war. Most political leaders are of the transactional type, where their decisions are dictated by events. Transformational leadership, on the other hand, is where massive changes are made by leaders whose desire to see change is not prompted by current events or circumstances but by a vision – a vision of where they want their nation to be. Soviet leader Mikhail Gorbachev was such a leader who saw *glasnost* and *perestroika* as the way forward for the Soviet people, which ultimately precipitated the end of the Cold War and the dissolution of the Soviet empire, something that Gorbachev himself had not intended.

Mikhail Sergeyevich Gorbachev (1931–) was the former general secretary of the Communist Party of the Soviet Union from 1985 and the last head of state of the USSR, having served from 1988 until its dissolution in 1991. Gorbachev was born in Stavropol Krai into a peasant Ukrainian-Russian family and graduated from Moscow State University in 1955 with a law degree. He became an active member of the Communist Party of the Soviet Union while he was at university. In 1979, he was appointed a member of the politburo, and within three years of the successive deaths of Soviet leaders Leonid Brezhnev, Yuri Andropov, and Konstantin Chernenko, Gorbachev rose to general secretary of the politburo in 1985. He was the first Soviet leader born during communist rule and represented a new generation of Soviet leadership.

Upon taking power in 1985, Gorbachev announced that the Soviet economy was stalled and that it needed to be revived with a programme of reform which was adopted by the central committee. Gorbachev quickly realised that the Soviet bureaucracy required urgent reforms of the political and social structures of the communist nation. One of his first acts was to introduce quality controls in the manufacturing sector to eliminate inferior products that were the hallmarks of communism and a lack of open market competition. Incredibly, Gorbachev's reforms were not meant as a transition to market socialism but a way to prop up the centrally planned economy. He was still a firm believer of socialism. In 1986, Gorbachev introduced the new policy of reconstruction called *perestroika*, which was an attempt to accelerate economic and social progress in the Soviet Union. The mechanisms he used to define *perestroika* were a combination of initiative and creative endeavour, improved order and discipline, and democracy within a socialist self-government. He went further in 1988 by introducing new freedoms to the Soviet people, which he referred to as *glasnost*, a radical change which allowed free speech and government criticism that was prohibited in the old Soviet system. Tight controls on the press were lifted, and thousands of dissidents and political prisoners were released. Gorbachev hoped that *glasnost* would entice the Soviet people to embrace his reform initiatives. He also hoped that *glasnost* would pressure conservatives who opposed his policies of economic restructuring to climb on board.

The most monumental of all of Gorbachev's foreign policy reforms was the dumping of the Brezhnev Doctrine, which effectively allowed the Eastern Bloc nations to freely determine their own internal affairs without interference from Moscow. On 6 July 1989, four months before the fall of the Berlin Wall and one month after Poland deposed its own communist government in free elections, Gorbachev declared before the Council of Europe in Strasbourg, 'The social and political order in some countries . . . is entirely a matter for each people to decide. Any attempt to limit the sovereignty of another state . . . would be inadmissible.' This was the trigger that set in motion a domino effect of revolts that spread from one Eastern European capital to another throughout 1989, which ousted pro-Soviet communist regimes that were built after World War II. Communism in Eastern Europe was finally overthrown, and the collapse of Soviet domination of Eastern Europe effectively ended the Cold war, for people under communist rule clearly understood that with equality forced upon them, they are not free. With communism gone, they were finally free.

Gorbachev's attempts at reform ended the political supremacy of the Communist Party of the Soviet Union and led to the dissolution of the Soviet Union. He was awarded the Nobel Peace Prize in 1990 for bringing about the end of the Cold War, something he had never anticipated when he assumed the reins of power over a stagnant USSR in 1985. Despite all this, Gorbachev was still a committed communist, albeit with a human face. Notwithstanding his revolutionary reforms, Gorbachev was eventually toppled from power by Boris Yeltsin, who finally marked the end of the Soviet Union and seventy years of communist rule. In his quest to reform his stagnant nation, Gorbachev inadvertently transformed it and, in the process, changed the whole geo-political map of Europe forever – quite a feat, no doubt, but not what he had originally intended. Oops!

***

In any strategy, simplicity is the ultimate sophistication which all leaders must strive for. It is easy to make things hard but hard to make them easy. People who are compensated to find complicated solutions lack the incentive to implement simplified ones. So it is not surprising that bureaucrats thrive on complexity because simplicity threatens their very existence. Therefore, it is essential not to end up blindly pursuing policies devised by top-level bureaucrats that appear good in theory but disastrous in practice. The trick is to ensure that you are surrounded and supported by people with common sense who are competent and reliable; otherwise, you may find yourself doing their job. U.S. president Lyndon B. Johnson made the mistake of getting himself too involved in the detailed bombing offensive of the Vietnam War instead of leaving the war details to his generals and looking at ways of ending the conflict, which was becoming highly unpopular at home. Johnson also strictly adhered to a hierarchical chain of command, which meant you could only communicate to the president via a mountain of bureaucratic layers. This resulted in highly filtered information reaching the president, which made it impossible for him to get a proper handle on the volatile issues that gripped America in the 1960s. As Johnson proved, a leader who is detached from the very people he leads will end up pursuing a flawed decision-making process with unpopular outcomes.

Unlike President Johnson, leaders should make it their responsibility to oversee the big issues facing their government and instruct subordinates to handle the details. Leadership is a special position that is rarely suited to those who tend to overthink things. An effective leader must step away from a management mindset and adopt a visionary role. Excessive attention to detail and constant interfering by leaders will only cause antipathy and lower morale. The simple advice is don't overmanage and overthink things to the point of paralytic inaction. U.S. president Jimmy Carter epitomised the dangers on focusing too much on the details, which made him an indecisive and ineffectual leader.

James Earl 'Jimmy' Carter Jr. (1924–) was the thirty-ninth president of the United States (1977–1981). Before he became president, Carter was a peanut farmer and naval officer and served for one term as governor of Georgia (1971–1975). Throughout his career, Carter was a strong advocate of human rights, and it has been widely considered that he was a better man than he was a president. At the start of his presidency, Carter seemed a sincere, honest, and well-meaning Southerner, but his administration suffered from his political naivety. He paid too much attention to detail, which stymied his ability to clearly define his priorities. Carter frequently appeared to be indecisive and was quick to retreat when under fire from political rivals, which made him appear weak. He seemed uninterested in working with others, including Congress, which, curiously, was controlled by his own party. Quite frankly, Carter really did sweat the small stuff and failed to delegate tasks to subordinates as his serious and introspective temperament demanded he see all the fine print before making decisions. Unfortunately, his personal attention to every detail may have been the root cause of his indecisiveness and apparent weakness in the public eye.

As a one-term president, Carter took office during a period of international stagflation, which persisted throughout his term. By the end of his presidential tenure, Carter's popularity was irreparably damaged by a terrible combination of the 1979–1981 Iran hostage crisis, the 1979 energy crisis, the Three Mile Island nuclear accident, and the Soviet invasion of Afghanistan in 1979. This made it easy for his opponent, Ronald Reagan, to portray him as a weak and ineffectual leader, causing Carter to become the first president since 1932 to lose a re-election bid. Sadly, Carter's presidency was largely considered a failure, and he will be remembered more for his post-presidency humanitarian work, which earned him the Nobel Peace Prize in 2002. The lesson from Jimmy Carter's presidency is that too much attention to detail overloads the decision-making process.

That's where leaders really need to rely on subordinates to check the details so that leaders can focus on the big picture.

A good political narrative is less about specifics and details and more about the big picture and vision. People who focus on the little details are masking a lack of any clear, coherent big thoughts. There is no point in focusing on the details when the big picture is a mess as the small things don't matter anyway. Don't do anything that someone else can do better. Focus on what you are good at and hire everyone else to do the rest. Great companies don't hire skilled people and motivate them. They hire already motivated people and inspire them. The best workers are those who collaborate with others, adapt to uncertainty, and are willing to learn. Give motivated workers something to believe in, something bigger than their job to work towards, and they will motivate themselves to work harder. Pulling a team together and giving them a cause to pursue ensures a greater sense of teamwork and camaraderie. You must instil a sense of purpose to your team and be open and honest and give them a voice in how things work. Quite often, it is not *what* a worker does that gets him out of bed every morning, but it's *why* he does it. Giving team members a sense of control and responsibility improves how much self-discipline they bring to their jobs – and don't forget that a rested worker is a more effective worker because productivity and long working hours do not go hand in hand as long workdays lead to more errors.

It is pointless recruiting the best people and restricting their ability to have any impact. The failure to delegate tasks to others depletes your energy as you try and take on too many activities that, in the end, never get done. Effective people leverage their activities by transferring responsibility to others who are better trained and more skilled at completing the task at hand. Your best workers must be valued and rewarded since a reward for improved performance works better than punishment for mistakes. Pick an area where your workers are frustrated and let them fix it. The effective delegation of duties produces a much bigger output because let's not forget the old saying that you buy time from someone with time to spare.

Efficient management without effective leadership is like straightening the deck chairs on a sinking ship. Management is about climbing the ladder of success, whilst leadership is about knowing where to position that ladder. Failure in leadership can never be compensated for by management success. It is interesting to observe how highly effective managers with successful careers in senior positions appear to flounder when they step up to the top job. They flounder because they cannot let go of their ingrained routine of dealing with details and micromanaging their staff. What many don't appreciate is that leadership is a whole new ball game that entails greater responsibility that cannot be handled alone. Good leaders need the support of a good team, and a good team needs the guidance of a good leader. As an analogy, a driver does not need to know every intricate engineering and technical detail to drive a car. Likewise, political leaders do not need to know every technical detail of the political machine; they just need to choose where they want to go and instruct the political machine to take them there. Political leaders need to be in the driver's seat, not in the engine room, and it is not just steering that leaders need to concentrate on. There is also the accelerator and brake pedal that need attention. Focusing too much on the minute details of day-to-day government activities runs the risk of overlooking the big issue items that leaders need to pay attention to. Intense focusing on a task can make political leaders effectively blind to the obvious. Make sure your people are working under optimum conditions that support, not hinder, their talents. The inability to delegate tasks and responsibilities is a sign of an insecure leader who lacks trust and confidence in others around him. Leaders need to temper their grip on power by sharing the burdens of high office with intelligent and trustworthy deputies.

When searching for workers to undertake the heavy lifting duties of office, always look for the dissatisfied, the unhappy, and the insecure as such people are riddled with weaknesses and have needs that you can fill. The bigger the task you ask of them to do, the more willing and able they will be. People's need for validation and recognition, their need to feel important, is the best kind of weakness to exploit. The insecure are suckers for any kind of social validation and, together with the unhappy, are people least able to disguise their weaknesses. Given the opportunity to tackle difficult tasks, good parliamentary staff will rise to the challenge and feel a sense of duty that will spur them on. Empowering your deputies to work independently, without your constant interference, gives them a sense of pride and duty to you. Leaders need to recognise that subordinates only thrive if they are given challenges and a variety of tasks that provides them a sense of responsibility, status, and control of their workload. When leaders find themselves taking on more jobs than they can possibly handle, their subordinates are left with little to do. Too little responsibility for the workers can result in stress, boredom, and lethargy, which are difficult to shake off. Delegating tasks to the most capable people frees up the leader to concentrate on important matters of national interest.

One of the biggest challenges of leadership is the feeling that there are just not enough hours in the day to get things done. All leaders have their own time managers who schedule their daily activities. However, experienced political leaders know that objectives and goals can change very rapidly in response to crises. A good leader should be able to prioritise his objectives and divide his workload according to the degree of urgency. The urgent task that requires his full and immediate attention may be a crisis in the economy, civil disobedience, or a policy blunder that has backfired and requires an urgent response. This is where top advisers are called in for immediate discussions on how the problem or task can best be handled. Leaders need to lean on their advisers to come up with solutions since a national crisis cannot be handled alone. The leader must squeeze every last drop of ideas from his trusted team before choosing the best option. Less urgent tasks or projects that need attention should be passed onto the people intimately involved in the project as they are usually in the best position to deal with them. Without the leader's drive, the project may lapse, so it is essential that a leader keeps their hands on the steering wheel and foot on the pedal to make sure the task is completed quickly. Routine low-priority projects or tasks can be given a kick along every now and then. A leader's time is precious. Checking on every fine detail of their subordinate's activities is a waste of time for a leader who has many important things to get on with.

Diversity in your team is essential because problems are best solved by a group of people with a broad range of knowledge and skills. Leaders just need to ensure that the staff have clear directions to follow and open lines of communication when advice is sought or problems arise. Workers should be encouraged to not come with a problem without offering a plan for how to solve it. Constant encouragement and a show of appreciation are more effective in maintaining loyalty and respect than harsh criticism and condemnation, which only alienates people. So don't sweat the fine details, but make sure you have reliable people who do. Learn to let go, but make sure you are kept fully informed and updated. Information is knowledge, and knowledge is power, so always seek it and never ignore it. However, as we shall see in the last chapter, loyalty can sometimes obstruct the free flow of crucial information.

CHAPTER 10

Loyalty and Who You Represent

Legend has it that the French general Napoleon Bonaparte had little need for sleep, and while on war expeditions, he spent his evenings walking around his camp, getting to meet and greet all his soldiers on a first-name basis. Napoleon had a great memory for names, and it certainly helped cultivate loyalty amongst his troops. Napoleon knew that his conquest of Europe required absolute loyalty from his troops since mass desertion was always a real problem that he had to contain and suppress through respect and trust. Hence, being respected as a commander is better than being liked.

Your power requires the support of others, who, in turn, are incentivised to stay loyal either through graft or perceived benefits that the leader provides in exchange for loyalty. It is not the loyalty of the voting public you seek but that of people who support your power base. Without the loyalty of your closest colleagues, your power base will crumble. Political leaders must always be mindful of the importance of loyalty to the strength and well-being of their leadership. Loyalty is nurtured by a bond of trust if leaders can maintain the confidence of their powerful backers. Great leaders want talent and strive to be loyal to their team as they expect their team to be loyal to them.

Staff are more productive when their leader is likable and easily approachable. Reverence is what leaders require to win loyalty, and being fair but firm is necessary to maintain loyalty. Feelings of duty, devotion, and attachment are the essence of loyalty. A good political leader cultivates an open-door policy so that deputies and subordinates can feel relaxed about sharing ideas and concerns with their leader. Devotion can only thrive if there are open channels of communication between the head office and the rest of the party. Productivity declines precipitously when leaders show no interest and build a formidable barrier between themselves and their subordinates. When this happens, leaders are effectively cut off and lose control of the government machinery that is crucial to the running of the country.

Disloyalty results in disunity. Dissent and discord amongst party members can ferment if the leader continually overlooks their views and ignores their opinions. A leader who is blind to the rumblings of his supporter base and disregards warning signs of discontent will leave himself exposed to damaging divisions within the party. Subordinates are more likely to do their own thing, often without the leader's knowledge or approval, if they feel intimidated and reluctant to approach their leader in times of need. Disloyalty leads to fickleness amongst supporters, which may trigger open revolt. We do not have to look too far back in history to find Kevin Rudd, Australia's former PM, who was toppled in 2010 after he failed the loyalty test by ignoring deputies and doing his own thing. In a democracy, a leader's power is dependent on the loyalty of their deputies. Once loyalty is lost, power is undermined, and the leader becomes a lame duck and a target to overthrow.

Leaders should avoid complacency when it comes to party loyalty and be aware that disloyalty can spread very quickly like a bushfire. If it is not put out early, disloyalty will become too hard to manage and result in the leader's demise. Paranoia arises when leaders cannot be certain of loyalty from their colleagues, which may be a real cause for concern or simply an anxious misconception. Either way, allegiance and devotion can be quite fickle in the world of politics, especially if there are other ambitious and conniving party members who have plans for the top job. It may be prudent to identify these threats early and test the loyalty of wavering party members in an open forum so that they can be kept in check. Excessive paranoia will often paralyse a leader who spends more time fearing their position than getting on with the business of government. So there must be a balance between getting on with the business of leadership and watching your back.

Political leaders who take the word of overconfident experts can expect costly consequences. On occasions, loyalty may be used as a surreptitious process for ambitious subordinates to gain favours and to fulfil hidden agendas. The secret to a clever political leader is their intuitive understanding of the play of human ambition and rivalry in their own party. A shrewd leader must be acutely aware of the power tussles amongst the deputies who strive to please their leader with their open display of loyalty. As we shall see, the smokescreen of loyalty can be a ploy that some ambitious subordinates may use to further their own agendas.

Social interactions are central to how humans harvest information and make decisions. When people are free to do as they please, they usually imitate one another. In the group setting, we unconsciously imitate what others are saying or doing because we are more concerned with fitting in to cement our sense of belonging. We adopt the ideas, beliefs, and values of the group so that we lose our rationality and independence of thought, which can be dangerous if the group is led by a mad cult figure. Sadly, loyalty can sometimes be blind and unquestioning, where the leader exploits it to commit atrocities in the name of faith, stability, and progress. Powerful personalities can undermine the wisdom of crowds because people will follow the herd mentality and fall behind them as it is more socially acceptable to agree than to dissent. Dissenting, after all, is hard work, especially if you are in the minority. It is easier to go along with group consensus even though some members may have doubts which they are reluctant to share because they want to belong.

Blind faith binds groups more strongly and provides comfort to their members who cannot accept harsh realities and prefer easy cures, romantic images, and other worldly experiences to their banal, common existence. Religious fervour, where followers develop an unquestioning devotion to their spiritual leader, is sometimes no different to a political leader with an ideology that sucks in an entire population. How many people would put their life on the line for their dear leader? Many, it seems, and Jim Jones, the charismatic leader of the Peoples Temple, was just such a case study worth a brief mention.

James Warren 'Jim' Jones (1931–1978) was the notorious founder and leader of the Peoples Temple and established Jonestown in Guyana as a model communist community. Like leaders of other communist regimes, Jones did not permit members to leave the community. He first established the Peoples Temple in Indiana in the 1950s and moved to California, setting up its headquarters in San Francisco in the 1970s. To avoid media scrutiny, he moved to Guyana and set up Jonestown as a 'socialist paradise' and a sanctuary from U.S. authorities who became concerned enough to send U.S. congressman Leo Ryan in November 1978 to investigate. Unfortunately, Ryan was killed as he tried to fly out with members of the sect who elected to leave with him and return to the United States.

The killing of the congressman and four of his party prompted Jones to order the mass murder/suicide of nine hundred temple members. It became the single greatest loss of American civilian lives in criminal history – that is, until 11 September 2001. If you think that's a lot of crazy people who were loyal enough to kill themselves, then spare a thought for a whole nation that followed their dear leader, Chairman Mao, with unquestioning loyalty and paid the ultimate price of up to seventy million deaths. The Stalinist USSR clearly showed how utopianism can quickly lead to totalitarianism. Totalitarian movements get their power from claims they are following 'nature and history' according to race (Nazi Germany) or class (the Bolshevik revolution) or religion (the Islamic State). In a totalitarian state, individual life means nothing, and the well-being of their own people is the least of their concerns as they foster or nurture their grand idea of world conquest. Blind loyalty, as we shall see below, does come with a heavy price.

Mao Zedong (1893–1976) or Mao Tse-tung or simply Chairman Mao was a leader of the Chinese Communist Revolution and founding father of the People's Republic of China from its establishment in 1949. He held absolute control over the entire nation until his death in 1976. In 1938, Mao Zedong proclaimed that 'political power grows out of the barrel of a gun', which reflected his ideology. He is remembered for Maoism, which refers to his military strategies and brand of policies as well as his theoretical interpretation of Marxism-Leninism. Mao is credited with leading the Long March and commanding the Communist Party of China to victory in the Chinese Civil War and, in the process, helped unify China as one nation. Mao also enacted policies which laid the economic, cultural, and technological foundations of modern China, transforming the country from a peasant-based farming society into a major industrialised world power.

Throughout the 1920s, Mao led several labour struggles, but he quickly realised that industrial workers were unable to lead the revolution because of their relatively small numbers, and so he turned to the rural Chinese peasants, who later became loyal supporters of his violent revolution. Coming from a peasant family himself, Mao built up his reputation amongst the farming peasantry and introduced them to communism. Mao relied on the need to win over the hearts and minds of the people to build up support in the countryside, which culminated in the successful rise of the Communist People's Republic of China in 1949. With the help of a tightly controlled media, Mao's image and that of the party were promoted to the Chinese people, who were exhorted to devote themselves to creating a strong nation of communists. Just to make sure that people got the message, Mao personally organised mass repressions and even established a system of execution quotas which he defended as a necessary means of securing power. Unyielding loyalty, it seems, was the order of the day.

Starting in 1951, Mao initiated two successive movements known as the three-anti/five-anti campaigns, where a reign of unrelenting terror came to pass as workers informed on their bosses, wives denounced their husbands, and children turned on their parents. The victims were often publicly humiliated and intimidated, and several hundreds of thousands committed suicide. Terrified people were reformed or sent to labour camps, while those who held out were shot. To root out critics, Mao cunningly introduced the Hundred Flowers Campaign, which gave people the freedom to express themselves and provide different opinions on how China should be governed. After a few months of harsh criticism, Mao's government reversed its policy and promptly persecuted those who spoke out. It seems that the policy was a clever tactic used to expose dissention within the population. The Hundred Flowers movement led to the condemnation and death of millions of citizens who were critical of the government. Mao Zedong had a personality cult that affected every aspect of Chinese life and was regarded as the undisputed head of China's working class. Mao's already glorified image manifested into a godlike figure who led China onto the path of power and strength as an independent nation. In his determination to fight against imperialism, feudalism, and capitalism, which were the three evils in pre-1949 China, Mao was responsible for a death toll that surpassed both Adolf Hitler and Joseph Stalin.

Mao's personality cult influenced several generations of Chinese people's way of life, and his image has become a symbol of revolutionary culture and totalitarianism. Mao's *Quotations From Chairman Mao Tse-Tung*, which was known as *The Little Red Book*, became mandatory reading, and party members were encouraged to carry a copy with them as a criterion for membership. Mao was literally worshipped like a god figure – loyalty at its most extreme. While he remains a controversial figure to this day,

Mao is officially held in high regard in China and is recognised as one of the one hundred most influential people of the twentieth century by the *Time* magazine. Between forty and seventy million deaths are attributed to Mao from his nationwide political campaigns such as the Great Leap Forward and the Cultural Revolution, which caused severe famine and widespread damage to culture, society, and the economy of China during his rule from 1949 to his death in 1976. Sadly, unquestioning loyalty can have tragic consequences for populations who are repressed and prevented from expressing their concerns.

Not only is blind loyalty just a burden for the population, but also, it can suppress the flow of vital information that political leaders need for effective decision making. A wonderful example is the hapless Jim Hacker MP, the fictional character of the BBC TV series *Yes Minister*, who relied on the scheming but superficially loyal Sir Humphrey Appleby for all his information. Sir Humphrey was effectively the gatekeeper for all the information that reached his minister and was able to manipulate the whole political process to his own advantage. Leaders must always look for information from sources beyond their closely woven network of loyal supporters because loyal followers can sometimes obstruct the free flow of vital information. If anything, loyalty may distort a leader's view of himself and the world around him. Deputies closest to the leader sometimes act as gatekeepers for information, like Sir Humphrey, and only convey information that they believe their leader wants to hear. Truth becomes the most serious casualty when loyal followers suppress discontent and dissatisfaction amongst the people and relay only positive news to their leader. Consequently, loyalty can be damaging if the information you need to govern your country is being filtered by your closest, most loyal deputies.

By barricading themselves with a few close loyal advisers, leaders run the risk of being fed filtered information that may be scrambled or inaccurate. In his efforts to please the Fuhrer, the World War II German air force commander Hermann Göring was notorious for feeding Hitler false information about the state of the air war during the Battle of Britain by hiding the true extent of losses incurred by the German Luftwaffe. Satisfied by Göring's reassurance that Britain had been subdued, the misinformation prompted Hitler to open a second front against the Russians with Operation Barbarossa, which triggered the beginning of the end of the Third Reich. While we are on the topic of Hitler and his Nazi Party, they have come to symbolise the power of evil which led many normal citizens to commit atrocities in the name of the 'Fatherland'. There is no doubt that a malevolent leader like Hitler could only execute his evil plans with the help of not only his close henchmen but also with the full cooperation of an entire nation. Evil, it seems, requires unquestioning loyalty, and Hitler was able to command absolute loyalty, which blinded a whole nation.

Another dangerous aspect of loyalty is found with larger-than-life leaders who only hire people or 'yes men' who agree with them. Unbridled egotism blinds a man to the realities around him, where he comes to live in a world of his own imagination with the feelings of 'I'm special', 'I'm better than everyone', and 'The rules don't apply to me'. They have an unhealthy belief in their own importance. They have a craving to be better than, have more than, and be recognised for. They are often ruthlessly determined to get their own way and are prepared to abandon the virtues of fairness, honesty, and integrity to achieve their aims. They are quick to blame others, including foreign powers, when things go wrong at home. Such shameless behaviour is often hidden behind a facade of well-honed charm. They surround themselves with yes men who clean up their messes and create a bubble in which they become disconnected from reality. Does this sound familiar? Let's take a look at a recent example of a larger-than-life personality who fits that description – former U.S. president Donald J. Trump.

As the forty-fifth president of the United States (2017–2021), Donald Trump is the only president in American history to have been impeached twice. During his four tumultuous years in office, Trump is best remembered for his record number of false statements and public misinformation campaigns that is unprecedented in American politics and has become a distinctive part of his political legacy. Trump's political positions have been variously described as nationalist, populist, isolationist, and protectionist. He has also been openly and unapologetically racist and misogynist and an extreme narcissist whom even communist and fascist dictators would find hard to beat. The Trump administration had a high turnover of personnel, and by the end of Trump's first year in office, 34 per cent of his original staff had resigned or been fired. As of early July 2018, 61 per cent of Trump's senior aides had left, which followed the departure of 141 staffers in the previous year. It was clear that loyalty was a major issue during Trump's presidency, and anyone who didn't follow Donald's command of strict obedience were shown the door.

Not surprisingly, Trump lost all sense of reality, which was reflected in his proclamation of fringe ideas and beliefs that had no basis whatsoever. Despite a campaign promise to eliminate national debt, Trump approved large increases in government spending, which he topped off with tax cuts in 2017. As a result, the federal budget deficit blew out to 50 per cent or nearly $1 trillion by 2019. On another front, Trump initiated a trade war in the expectation that it would revive American manufacturing and the reshoring of factory production, both of which never materialised. Instead, Trump left office with three million fewer U.S. jobs than when he took office, which makes Trump the only U.S. president in modern history to leave office with a smaller workforce.

His biggest failure as U.S. president – and what he will always be remembered for – was his poor handling of the COVID-19 pandemic. With infections and deaths continuing to rise, Trump adopted his signature strategy of blaming the states for the growing pandemic rather than accepting that his views of the pandemic were inept and overly optimistic. As the pandemic worsened and amid criticism of his failure to provide presidential leadership, Trump refused to admit any mistakes in his handling of the outbreak, instead blaming democratic state governors, the previous administration, the media, WHO, and, of course, China. Just to really show how badly he had lost control of the situation, Trump said several times that the United States would have fewer cases of the coronavirus if it did less testing and that having many reported cases 'makes us look bad'. His disinformation about the pandemic significantly weakened and delayed the national response to it, which resulted in one of the highest death rates from the coronavirus in the Western world that surpassed the U.S. mortality figures from the Spanish flu almost a century ago.

Trump completed his term as U.S. president in 2021 with a record-low approval rating of between 29 per cent and 34 per cent, the lowest of any U.S. president. In one of his last acts as U.S. president, he incited angry mobs to storm the Capitol building, which confirmed his place in history as that of a leader who demanded and expected unyielding loyalty that resulted in chaos and anarchy right to the very end. The turmoil of the Donald Trump presidency is a pertinent reminder of the importance of limited terms placed on leaders in Western democracies.

Trump had all the traits of an extreme narcissist who has a need for admiration with a lack of empathy and displayed attention-seeking behaviour. He was hypersensitive to any perceived slight or criticism and was a master at turning the tables and making others feel guilty. Everything Trump said or did was for public consumption, which was displayed by continual drama and the theatrical quality of his gestures, which were made for television. To his followers, Trump was a cult figure who emphasised the visual and sensual over the intellectual, which amused the bored and scared off the cynics. To maintain their allegiance, Trump created an 'us versus them' dynamic. Having a large following opened up all sorts of possibilities for deception – not only will followers worship their cult leader, but also, they will defend him from his enemies, which partly explains the storming of the Capitol building.

Loyalty has an emotional element that may contain the seeds of destruction if not carefully monitored. While most modern leaders do not desire or care for a Chairman Mao style of public devotion, they must be careful not to smother themselves with loyal supporters who may suffocate the decision-making process. Loyalty is a high priority, but access to good information must be an even higher priority. So it pays to keep loyalty in perspective and demand access to raw information from independent sources. It is a well-known fact that those who control the flow of information are the real masters of the universe. This type of loyalty – feeding only information that leaders want to hear – destroys a leader's ability to make an informed judgement and paralyses the decision-making process to the detriment of the nation. When everyone agrees, there is a good chance that there isn't enough diversity in your information and sources of ideas. Seeing a situation from a variety of viewpoints helps develop better solutions to problems. Otherwise, relying on a few loyal deputies for information is like using only the touch of your fingertips to make sense of the world around you.

***

In the golden age of monarchy, people were subjects, not citizens. The king or queen was their protector, their sovereign ruler, not their representative. It was a hierarchical society presided over by a monarch, where everyone knew their place. In an age where violence ruled, stability was strongly guarded at the expense of other values such as liberty and justice. Social stability and moral order were maintained by unquestioning loyalty to the crown. In other words, it was like one big protection racket – you simply pay your taxes and show loyalty to your monarch, and you won't get hurt. If you had a grievance, then it was tough luck. Your king or queen would be too busy fighting foreign wars to care about the poor condition of the roads around your village. Those were the days when it was a privilege to be a subject of the realm and it was an honour to serve your monarch. For someone living in the Middle Ages, it would be unfathomable to believe that just a few centuries later, the privilege of serving becomes a function of political leaders, and their masters are the very citizens whose support is critical to their power. While modern politics is a product of history which has swung away from hereditary rule in favour of universal representation, there are still parts of the modern world, in particular Russia, where leaders only pay lip service to the virtues of democracy.

What the people give can also take away. Your constituents expect that you have their best interests at heart and that you will represent them to the best of your abilities. In previous chapters, I briefly discussed incentives and their importance in electing people to leadership roles. Essentially, people are selfish and will support anyone who promises prosperity at minimal cost. A basic premise of politics is that individual personalities and how they interrelate are what drive the political process. The interests of individuals must be carefully balanced with the interests of society. Democracy is about representation, but who you represent is often not all that clear. It may appear on the surface that your allegiance lies with the people who voted for you at the general election, but as we shall see, your allegiance lies with your party and specifically those in your party who have the power and influence to fulfil your leadership ambitions. In other words, it is the dominant political parties, with their various powerful factions, that determine who gets what.

Politics is the curious logic of exploitation of the many by the few because the few with lots to gain will fight, campaign, and lobby much harder than the millions of citizens who each have little to lose. The smaller the social group or class, the more focused it can be on asserting and maintaining its power to the exclusion of others. In effect, it is the unified elites who dominate the disorderly masses. In Europe, farmers make up a tiny portion of the population, yet they command more subsidies than any other group. India, on the other hand, has a large agricultural sector, yet it receives few government subsidies, which are mainly directed to the nascent technological industries that are small in comparison. It seems that strength in numbers does not count as much as a loud, well-organised voice with a direct line to the government.

So how do political leaders balance the broader needs of their communities without upsetting boisterous pressure groups? The loud calls of radical environmental groups to save forests from the logging industry, which is the lifeblood of local townships, is a precarious balance between ideology and jobs. It is a no-brainer to work out that if the environmentalists lose the fight, they simply move on to another cause, but if loggers lose the fight, they lose their livelihoods, and the whole town goes into terminal decline. Political leaders are expected to do the right thing, and this boils down to protecting the economic livelihood of the nation. When it comes to issues which pit activists against workers, politicians simply follow the votes, like a business follows profits. Fortunately, the decision is often made by the political party you represent. In other words, if the main support base of your political party comes largely from an inner-city electorate, environmental issues should be a high priority. If your party represents rural electorates, then jobs are your number one consideration. Let's examine this closer.

The demographics of key electorates that form the basis of support for political parties dictate party policies. Rural areas demand job security and basic infrastructure such as sealed roads, sewerage, and reliable telecommunications. Outer suburban electorates are resolute on public transport and amenities such as schools, healthcare, and community centres. They constitute the marginal electorates where major political parties slug it out for control of these swinging seats. Middle suburban electorates demand housing affordability, so their main concerns are interest rates on mortgages, which depend on a sound economy. These electorates are inclined to support conservative political parties. Inner-city dwellers are often a mixed bunch, and they range from young left-leaning single people with idealistic views of the world and concern for the environment to older empty-nesters living in fashionable inner-city apartments who regard safety as their highest priority. In the middle, there are the public housing residents who rely on welfare, so their major concern would be the level of government handouts.

Successful political parties look for a comfortable middle ground that respects diverse community needs by appealing to a sense of fairness, rather than giving in to everyone's demands, which is impossible to do. So with that in mind, one of the greatest challenges of politics is trying to decide how to target votes. The rule of thumb embraced by socially conscious politicians is to make decisions that benefit most people. Unfortunately, this is often impractical as factional pressures, lobby groups, media interests, and the specific needs of the politician's own constituents rarely agree. Not surprisingly, it's impossible for political leaders to implement decisions that will satisfy everyone. For instance, increased funding to the arts may well attract favourable media attention, but it means little to a factory worker with rotten teeth who cannot afford basic dental care – a less glamorous issue, no doubt. In peacetime, increased spending on defence makes little sense to rural folks who have no basic healthcare facilities or properly sealed roads in their townships. There is, however, a way to overcome this dilemma.

Ironically, when people are free to do as they please, they usually imitate one another, so it may well be possible to sway large populations by focusing your energy on key opinion or community leaders. When we feel like we belong, we feel connected, and we feel safe. We all want to be around people and organisations who are like us and share our beliefs. It makes us feel wanted, loved, and protected above members of other tribal groups. Belonging to a tribe or group supplies that sense of social solidarity, and the key opinion or community leaders of these group have immense influence which needs to be tapped by aspiring politicians seeking votes.

Another way to garner votes is to drive people out of their comfort zones by cultivating dissatisfaction, frustration, or anger at the current state of affairs. When anger takes over from cynicism and despair, revolution is in the air, and votes are more likely to favour the challenger over the incumbent. Politicians simply go where the political process takes them, and that means they may back policies that are likely to attract more votes, even if it is not in the best interests of the community. For example, focusing on high crime rates, whether real or imagined, is a sure-fire way to attract the voting public's attention. One unfortunate example of political vote buying is the preference for more prisons so they appear tough on crime, and yet if those funds were diverted to mental health and drug and alcohol programmes, there would be far less need for prisons. Essentially, appearing tough seems to attract votes, while prevention programmes appear weak and unappetising to voters.

Political party policies reflect an ideology that appeals to a core demographic profile. The key to a successful political party is to broaden its appeal to entice the support of the non-aligned voters. This is critical, especially for marginal seats where the bulk of the electioneering spectacle takes place. In a tight election, every swinging seat is crucial to all parties. True representation is only possible with independent political candidates because major parties follow a basic ideology that only allows for minor variations to satisfy the swinging voters. Independent politicians, on the other hand, are free from the shackles of party ideology and can focus on the local issues of their constituents by supporting policies that may have direct or indirect benefits for the people they represent. Under normal circumstances, independents have very little influence over policy matters. However, in a close election where the major parties score an equal number of seats, the independents become the kingpins and hold the balance of power. Effectively, the independents suddenly become important players by holding to ransom the major parties who covet their support.

Political power now resides with the independents, who must decide which party will form a government with their support. Concessions are extracted, and the big winners are the constituents represented by the independents, who stand to benefit from the lopsided symbiotic relationship between their independent representative and the government. The independents Oakeshott, Wilkie, Katter, and Jones did just that when they found themselves in the enviable position of being courted by the major parties after the tight Australian federal election result of June 2010. Both major parties were desperate for their support, but Labour's Gillard government was able to grant more concessions to the independents than the coalition. As far as the major parties are concerned, kowtowing to independents is not an attractive or desirable position to be in. That is why marginal electorates become the main battlegrounds at each election so that parties can secure enough seats to govern in their own right.

Despite the importance of marginal seats, these are often contested by junior politicians. Politicians who hold marginal seats need to make sure they visit their electorate often enough to reassure their constituents that they have not been forgotten. Otherwise, it just takes a very small swing of less than 6 per cent against them for the politicians to find themselves out in the wilderness at the next election. Ironically, even though marginal seats are largely given to junior party members to contest, they attract more publicity and election funds than any other seats. Contesting marginal seats gives junior politicians the opportunity to cut their political teeth. Safe seats are the province of senior ministers and cabinet for very good reasons. High-ranking politicians are invariably given safe seats where the populace dutifully aligns itself to a major party for a predictable outcome at every election. This is a convenient arrangement because senior ministers cannot devote the time and energy for grass-roots political favours when they must concentrate on the nation as a whole. For those fortunate enough to hold safe seats, which usually include all senior ministers, the electorate aligns itself to the party so that even if your neighbour's pet chimpanzee stood as a candidate, they would win the election if they belonged to the right party. For these reasons, the nation's leaders are shielded by their party machine with a safe electoral seat, which means they are free to pursue policies that reflect their party's ideology.

While politicians are elected by the people, who and what they represent is inextricably linked to their political party's philosophies, beliefs, and principles. With few exceptions, people generally vote for political parties, not individuals. So if you are endorsed as the candidate for a major political party, you are guaranteed a substantial proportion of the votes, even if you decide to ditch the campaign and take an overseas holiday during the weeks leading up to the election. It is the party behind you that makes all the difference, so if political power is on your agenda, make sure you sign up to one of the major political parties. It is a pertinent reminder that political leaders, such as PMs and presidents, rarely come from outside the major political parties.

Leaders are a product of their political party. They represent not the common man on the street but the interests of their party. So leaders should be under no illusion as to where their powers come from as it is made all too clear when leaders are unceremoniously dumped from their leadership role by their own party machine, who decide whether they are toeing the party line. In a leadership tussle, it's not the voting public you need to convince but the prevailing factions and powerbrokers within your own party who decide who steps up to the leader's podium.

While elections determine who is in power, they do not determine how the power is used. That is up to the governing party to establish. The voting public are largely side-lined until the next election, and don't forget that you represent your party and you do what they tell you to do if you want to achieve your quest for political power. Good luck!

EPILOGUE

The complexities of modern society demand that politicians are well versed and comfortable with decisions that support progress and change that benefit the nation. One of the major problems of democracy is that long-term decisions and plans are rarely considered because the election cycle is too short to implement policies that would benefit societies in the long term. Political leadership in developed nations is a transient phenomenon, so monumental changes that improve society and the lives of its people require radical decisions that need to be implemented within the relatively short life of a government or administration. So think of political power as a transient phenomenon where you are given only a limited time in which to make a difference to your world.

Your legacy will depend on what actions you take during your limited time at the top. Therefore, before embarking on the road to political power, make sure you are doing it for all the right reasons and not just for the fame and glory. Politics is a tough gig, so you need to appreciate all the sacrifices that you will need to make along the way and what your unique contribution to the betterment of your nation, state, company, or organisation will be. If you think you have what it takes to make a difference to the world, then hopefully, this book will provide the essential roadmap you need to follow to succeed in your quest.

Now that we have travelled the long and tortuous road to political power, let's take a brief look back on the twelve guiding principles that we have visited along the roadmap:

1. To begin with, your appearance and oratorical skills are what bring you to the attention of the masses.

---

2. Shyness is not a desirable attribute in politics, but humility is. Dysfunctional personalities rarely survive for very long in the top job unless they resort to violence and repression.
3. Crafting and nurturing interpersonal relationships are critical to political survival as political leaders must rely on the trust and loyalty of others to succeed.
4. A fractious party cannot govern, so make sure you lead a united team.
5. Sometimes the truth can be damaging, so shrewd politicians need to work out effective ways to hide the truth behind clever words.
6. Never make rash decisions and bold statements that you may later come to regret as it is very hard to undo the damage that is done.
7. The media are your window to the people, so make sure you are always on your best behaviour.
8. Pay attention to the big picture and surround yourself with reliable and capable people who can take care of the fine details.
9. Refrain from personal attacks on other people as the public expect you to focus on policies. Strong policies are your tickets to govern.
10. Set the political agenda by planting the seeds of ideas that will arouse the public's attention.
11. Loyalty is important, but be careful not to build yourself a fortress of loyal supporters who may stymie the flow of important information that you need to govern.
12. While you represent the people, your allegiance lies with your political party, who can make or break political aspirations.

While the political landscape has changed considerably since Machiavelli's time, the fundamental issues of loyalty, willpower, and strength of resolve are still essential ingredients that political aspirants require to pursue leadership roles. Successful leaders rely on their strength of personality to help them climb the tortuous and slippery road to power. They devote the best years of their lives to endure the vicious political game of character assassination, lies and deceit, and the sacrifice of quality family time to gain political power. Political power, as we have seen, can be rather tenuous at best as friendships are usually based on convenience and relationships can be fleeting. However, despite all the negativity associated with politics, the ability to change the world in which we live is the greatest reward that political power brings, which surpasses all other vocations.

BIBLIOGRAPHY

Chapter 1

Machievelli's The Prince. *Niccolò Machiavelli & William J. Connell (Editor & Translator).*
Publ: Bedford/St. Martins, 1ˢᵗ Ed. (2005)
Politics: A Treatise on Government. *Aristotle.*
Publ: CreateSpace (2010)
Mugabe: Power, Plunder, and the Struggle for Zimbabwe's Future. *Martin Meredith.*
Publ: Public Affairs (2007)
Ivan the Terrible: Tsar of Death. *Sean Price.*
Publ: Franklin Watts, Reprint Ed. (2008)
Stalin: A Biography. *Robert Service.*
Publ: Belknap Press of Harvard University Press (2006)
Hitler: A Biography. *Ian Kershaw.*
Publ: W. W. Norton & Company (2010)
Antony Eden: A Biography. *Robert Rhodes James.*
Publ: McGraw-Hill (1987)
Henry VIII: The King and his Court. *Alison Weir.*
Publ: Ballantine Books (2002)

Chapter 2

Warren G. Harding. *John W. Dean.*
Publ: Times Books (2004)
Absolute Power: The Helen Clark Years. *Ian Wishart.*
Publ: Howling (2009)
Recollections of a Bleeding Heart. Paul Keating PM. *Don Watson.*

Publ: Random House Australia (2002)
Mass Media and American Politics. *Doris A. Graber.*
 Publ: C. Q. Press, 8th Ed. (2009)
The Diana Chronicles. *Tina Brown.*
 Publ: Anchor (2008)
Silvio Berlusconi: Television, Power, and Patrimony. *Paul Ginsborg.*
 Publ: Verso (2005)

Chapter 3
Gandhi — An Autobiography: The Story of My Experiments with Truth.
 Mahatma Gandhi,
Mahadeu Desai, & Sissela Bok.
Publ: Beacon Press (1993)
Mandela: A Biography. *Martin Meredith.*
Publ: Public Affairs, Reprint Ed. (2011)
Hawke: The Prime Minister. *Blanche D'Alpuget.*
Publ: Melbourne University Press (2010)

Chapter 4
Kennedy: The Classic Biography. *Theodore C. Sorensen.*
 Publ: Harper Perennial (2009)
Trotsky: A Biography. *Robert Service.*
 Publ: Belknap Press of Harvard University Press (2009)
The Age of Reagan: The Conservative Counterrevolution 1980–1989.
 Steven F. Hayward.
 Publ: Three Rivers Press, Reprint Ed. (2010)

Chapter 5
The Latham Diaries. *Mark Latham.*
 Publ: Melbourne University Press (2006)
The Science and Politics of Global Climate Change: A Guide to the
 Debate. *Andrew Dessler &   Edward Parson.*
 Publ: Cambridge University Press, 2nd Ed. (2010)
J. Edgar Hoover: The Man and the Secrets. *Curt Gentry.*
 Publ: W. W. Norton & Company (2001)
Thatcher and Thatcherism. *Eric J. Evans.*
 Publ: Routledge, 2nd Ed. (2004)

Kevin Rudd: An Unauthorized Political Biography. *Nicholas Stuart.*
  Publ: Scribe Publications Pty. Ltd. (2008)

Chapter 6
Robert Menzies: A Life. *A. W. Martin.*
  Volume 1: 1894–1943 Publ: Melbourne University Press (1996)
  Volume 2: 1944–1978 Publ: ACLS Humanities E-Book (2009)
Franklin Delano Roosevelt. *Alan Brinkley.*
  Publ: Oxford University Press (2009)
President Nixon: Alone in the White House. *Richard Reeves.*
  Publ: Simon & Schuster (2002)
Doctor Goebbels: His Life and Death. *Roger Manvell & Heinrich Fraenkel.*
  Publ: Skyhorse Publishing (2010)
A Failed Empire: The Soviet Union in the Cold War from Stalin to
  Gorbachev. *V. M. Zubok.*
  Publ: The University of North Carolina Press (2008)

Chapter 7
Saddam Hussein: A Biography. *Shiva Balaghi.*
  Publ: Greenwood (2008)
Gallipoli. *Peter Hart.*
  Publ: Oxford University Press (2011)
Lazarus Rising. *John Howard.*
  Publ: Harper Collins (2011)
The Survivor: Bill Clinton in the White House. *John F. Harris.*
  Publ: Random House Trade Paperbacks (2006)

Chapter 8
Naked Economics: Undressing the Dismal Science. *Charles Wheelan.*
  Publ: W. W. Norton, 2nd ed. (2010)
Hugo Chavez: Oil, Politics, and the Challenge to the U.S. *Nikolas Kozloff.*
  Publ: Palgrave Macmillan (2007)
Greenpeace: How a Group of Ecologists, Journalists, and Visionaries
  Changed the World. *Rex   Wayler.*
  Publ: Rodale Books (2004)
Think and Grow Rich. *Napoleon Hill.*
  Publ: Tribeca Books (2011)

Lincoln. *David Herbert Donald.*
    Publ: Simon & Schuster (1996)

Chapter 9
Transforming Leadership. *James MacGregor Burns.*
    Publ: Grove Press (2004)
Deng Xiaping and the Transforming of China. *Ezra Vogel.*
    Publ: Belknap Press of Harvard University Press (2011)
Churchill. *Paul Johnson.*
    Publ: Penguin (Non-Classics), Reprint Ed. (2010)
Gorbachev's Gamble: Soviet Foreign Policy and the End of the Cold War.
    Andrei Grachev.
    Publ: Polity (2008)
Lyndon B. Johnson: Portrait of a President. *Robert Dallek.*
    Publ: Oxford University Press (2005)
Don't Sweat the Small Stuff at Work. *Richard Carlson.*
    Publ: Hyperion (1998)
Jimmy Carter: A Comprehensive Biography from Plains to Post-Presidency.
    Peter G. Bourne.
    Publ: Scribner (1997)

Chapter 10
Loyalty: The Vexing Virtue. *Eric Felten.*
    Publ: Simon & Schuster (2011)
Raven: The Untold Story of the Rev. Jim Jones and his People. *Tim
    Reiterman.*
    Publ: Tarcher (2008)
Mao Zedong: A Life. *Jonathan D. Spence.*
    Publ: Penguin (Non-Classics) (2006)
The Oxford Illustrated History of the British Monarchy. *John Cannon &
    Ralph Griffiths.*
    Publ: Oxford University Press, 2nd ed. (2001)
Australian Politics for Dummies. *Nick Economou & Zareh Ghazarian.*
    Publ: Wiley Publishing Australia Pty. Ltd. (2011)